From Start to Stardom

BY LISA LONDON, CSA

With Rochell Goodrich

WHAT DO HOLLYWOOD INSIDERS SAY ABOUT THIS BOOK

"Best book EVER! Lisa really gives us the inside track on how to make it as an actor! There's so much to learn when getting started in Hollywood and this book is smart, concise and very insightful! A TRUE must have for every parent and actor!"

Tish Cyrus (Miley's Mom)

"As both an Actor and Executive Producer, I think Lisa's book is fantastic! She really explains the process of casting so an actor can understand what they need to do. As a former 3-Time NBA World Champion, I know a winner when I see one. 'From Start to Stardom' is your key to a successful career."

Rick Fox – Actor and Executive Producer

"Lisa London is a phenomenal resource for any actor, both new and seasoned, and her book is a wonderful tool and must-have for those wanting to know what's what in the entertainment industry."

Sarah Shyn, Manager - 3 Arts Entertainment

"Lisa's book "From Start to Stardom" is an invaluable and amazing tool for actors of any age. I have known Lisa London for 20 years and she is a true gift to the entertainment business. Lisa is a wealth of information and she is one of the few people in Hollywood that cares."

Cindy Osbrink, Owner/ Agent, The Osbrink Agency

"What a great book - Lisa tells it like it is. I followed much of her advice and ended up making my dream come true of being on a Disney Channel series."

Adam Irigoyen - (Shake It Up)

"I wish this book was available when I graduated from college and started auditioning. It's so great to hear this advice from a casting director's perspective. And Lisa is the best! I should know - she gave me my first television job and we've been friends ever since!"

Megan Hilty – (Smash, Wicked on Broadway)

"From Start to Stardom gives the actor something you CAN'T BUY or TEACH and that's HOPE."

Marv Dauer – (Marv Dauer Management)

FROM START TO STARDOM

ISBN-13: 978-1493771448
ISBN-10: 1493771442

DEDICATION

For my Mom and Dad who have always given me unconditional love and support. To my Mom who has always been there for me when any situation arises and to my Dad who is and always will be my hero. Thank you for introducing me to show business and to casting, I will be forever grateful.

To all aspiring actors, this book is for you.

Let your journey begin!

IMPORTANT NOTE TO THE READERS OF THIS BOOK

Please visit our website at **www.fromstarttostardom.com** where additional resources and information intended for book readers only are password protected. On our website you will find Lisa London's Q & A, expanded worksheets, large format color headshot examples, sample resumes and more information that could be of use to the aspiring actor.

Your password to gain access to these resources is:

start2stardom with no spaces and all lower case as shown.

FROM START TO STARDOM

CONTENTS

CHAPTER	TITLE	PAGE
	Acknowledgments	ix
	Special Introduction by Adrian R'Mante	x
	Introduction: I Like Actors	xii
1	Purpose	1
2	You've Decided This Is For You	5
3	Headshots	14
4	Resumes	35
5	How to Get Discovered and Promoting Yourself	44
6	The Role of Agents and Managers	57
7	Getting an Agent or Manager	73
8	Working With An Agent or Manager	86
9	Preparing for Your Audition	91
10	Going To Your Audition	105
11	Delivering Your Audition	117
12	What Happens When You Get the Job	133
13	Behind The Casting Director's Doors	136
14	Personal Attitude for Parents &/or Guardians	142
15	Achieving Your Goals	148
ii	About the Author	152
Index 1	Legal Information for Minors	153
Index 2	Additional Internet Resources	160
Index 3	Navigating Los Angeles	162

ACKNOWLEDGMENTS

To **Rochell Goodrich** for her inspiration, love and long term friendship and in making sure that we stayed on track and got this book completed. For helping write this book and for making this dream into a reality, it is truly appreciated.

To **George Goodrich** for his creative ideas in making my vision come true. For the cover, the layout of the book and all your creative genius.

To **Catherine Stroud** who has been my business colleague for twenty years in **London/Stroud Casting**. We have had many fun and exciting adventures together in casting. A lot of the actors that I talk about in this book we discovered together. Thank you for having a fantastic eye for talent and for being a great friend.

To **Pamela Fisher, Bonnie Liedtke, Rich Correll, Jason Earles, Sabrina** and **Beth Carpenter, Karon Hetherington** and **Lacy Brennan** for their insightful interviews and information that contributed to the book.

To **Brad Buckman** for his wonderful expertise in creating the photographs in our book and his awesome interview that I know will educate and inspire actors. Also, for being a great ping pong player. We need a rematch!

To **Meg Delacey, Cassie Brennan, Collin Levin, Juliocesar Chavez** and **Kaden Hetherington** for being the do's and don'ts of headshots.

To all the **Agents** and **Managers** who have brought London/Stroud Casting amazing talent over the years. I truly appreciate all your hard work and persistence.

To **Geoff Levin** for all your encouragement and support through-out my career.

To **Karen Renna** for being a true friend and encouraging us through this journey.

To **Jane Covner** for giving us great feedback and notes and for letting us know we were on the right track and to **Becky Whitt** for your superlative editing.

To **Vicki Southard-Town, Linda Lorch, Kelly Hare** and **Ethelda Worthy** for your awesome advice, guidance and friendship of many years.

To **Mike Brown** for giving us great notes on our final draft and for being a longtime family friend.

Lastly, to my children, **Collin** and **Savannah** who make me laugh everyday and for inspiring me to be a better mom. I couldn't have done this without your love and support.

SPECIAL INTRODUCTION: LISA LONDON CHANGED MY LIFE
By Adrian R'Mante

I wish I had this book when I was first starting out. Most of the information Lisa gives in this book I had to learn the hard way. For six years beginning in 1999 I was a struggling actor in Hollywood, getting the occasional and often uncredited bit part in a movie or TV show. I'd go out on numerous auditions and call-backs and mostly get passed over, but – and this is important – <u>I never gave up on my dream to be a professional, successful, working actor.</u>

I grew up in a dirt trailer park in Brandon, Florida, a small town outside of Tampa. I was a little Mexican kid in a neighborhood where we were among the most minor of minorities. I started my entertainment career as a break dancer. In high school, I was fortunate to have a drama teacher who thought I had talent and encouraged me. I wanted to leave for New York or Los Angeles immediately, but he wisely told me to train, practice and prepare myself to compete in New York or LA, where the talent pool is comprised of the best of the best. Lisa also stresses the importance of preparation throughout this book.

Lisa London changed my life by deciding to cast me as *Estebon*, a hotel bellman in the Disney TV Series, *The Suite Life of Zack and Cody*. Luck and timing was part of it, but that's not the whole story by any means. I had learned from every audition I went on, from other actors, teachers and coaches and by the time I went out on that fateful audition with Lisa, I was a better prepared and more professional actor than I would have been had she auditioned me just a year earlier.

Being on a successful TV series catapults one onto a whole new level professionally. I've had the opportunity to work with actors like **Al Pacino, Patrick Stewart, Jennifer Garner, Kelsey Grammer, Kiefer Sutherland** and **Gary Sinise** just to name a few.

Teaching is my other passion. Before *Suite Life* I had worked as a 9th and 10th grade English teacher. When *Suite Life* stopped filming, I combined my passions for acting and teaching by developing a TV and Film Acting Program through which I've helped train hundreds of talented kids. I love teaching young, up and coming actors on the many lessons I've learned on my road to success. One of those lessons is that if you are serious about becoming a professional actor, buy and read *From Start to Stardom* and maybe Lisa London can help change your life too.

AUTHOR'S INTRODUCTION: I LIKE ACTORS

Actor's performances have always inspired me. The question I often asked myself is, "Who will be the next star?" because I'm always looking for the next star.

I was born in Los Angeles and grew up in Hollywood. As a young girl I tagged along with my dad, Director, **Jerry London**, as often as possible. I loved being on the television sets with him. As a director of some of the most well known shows of that era, he knew everyone, or at least that's how it seemed to me. He directed *Hogan's Heroes, The Partridge Family, The Brady Bunch, Happy Days, The Mary Tyler Moore Show, Rockford Files, Kojak, Six Million Dollar Man, Wheels, Chiefs* and *Shogun* to name a few. He was the most notable Hollywood Director for Television and mini-series during my formative years.

Not only did I get to visit exotic locations, but I got to observe some of the greatest acting talents of all time. Wonderful actors like, **Gregory Peck, Christopher Plummer, Rock Hudson, Jane Seymour, Richard Chamberlain, Mary Tyler Moore, Bill Cosby, James Garner, Edward James Olmos, Shirley Jones, Florence Henderson, Telly Savalas** and **Danny Glover** were just a few of the incredible actors I was able to watch. Their journeys of how they became successful were fascinating to me. I'm not sure when it happened exactly, but I vowed to be part of this exciting business, myself.

Casting was a natural progression for me and it has been a great profession considering my lifelong connection to Hollywood.

We have all heard the stories of actors being discovered in places you would least expect, such as **Matt Dillon** who was discovered by a talent scout who spotted him hanging out in a hallway at his junior high school or **Jennifer Lawrence** who was discovered while vacationing in New York City. **Natalie Portman** was discovered while going out for pizza, and **Harrison Ford** got his big break while working as a carpenter for **George Lucas**. As he was building cabinets for Lucas' new office, George asked him to read lines for absent actors starring in his upcoming film, *Star Wars*. The rest is history!

Being "discovered" is just a part of the journey. Being prepared is a journey of its own! I wrote this book to assist **YOU** in navigating your career. In this day and age there are so many avenues for actors to showcase their talents. There are so many additional ways to promote yourself, get work and get discovered.

In addition to film, television and theater, people are being discovered every day through the ever-expanding internet media such as YouTube, Netflix, Amazon, Yahoo, Hulu and Web series.

In this book, I take you behind the Casting Director's doors, walking you step by step from getting started, to making the most of your headshot and resume, getting an agent and/or manager and much more. I include how to start promoting yourself and exact steps on how to get the part when auditioning. In some chapters, there are even worksheet pages for you to follow so you can get practical experience.

Also included are interviews with working Hollywood Professionals, including a top agent for young talent, an accomplished manager who has worked with leading actors and actresses of our time, and a Director of many successful television shows.

Anyone who has a dream to act deserves a chance to audition, so I want to share my knowledge and give aspiring actors the road to success. I wish you all the best in your journey.

Go to our website for more information or look for me on social media.

FROM START TO STARDOM

PURPOSE

You can't succeed at a game if you don't know the rules. I have over 20 years of experience in the business of casting children, teens and young adults for Television and Film. In the following chapters, I'm going to give you an insider's look at what I believe you need to know and understand in order for you, your child or teenager (or any actor) to have a real chance for success in the entertainment industry. But first—let's see if this game is really for you and/or your child.

Why Go On This Adventure?

We have written two sets of questions, one for the aspiring actor and one for the parents or guardian of the aspiring actor. Both of you should answer your own set of questions.

This is your workbook. Feel free to mark it up and write in it. You can begin by putting an actual check mark next to the possible answers listed on the next pages. I've also included practical exercises throughout the book to help you apply what you are learning.

ASPIRING ACTORS QUESTIONS:

1. Do people stop you all the time and tell you how funny/beautiful/talented you are?

____YES   ✓ NO

2. Do you watch television or movies and fantasize that you are in that show or movie?

✓ YES   ____NO

3. Are you always singing, dancing and performing for (yourself) or others?

✓ YES   ____NO

4. Are you always performing at family gatherings?

____YES   ✓ NO

5. Are you always talking about what you are going to do when you become a star?

____YES   ✓ NO

6. Are you always imitating voices and people from movies and television?

✓ YES   ____NO

7. Is acting what you dream about every day?

✓ YES   ____NO

8. Do you see yourself being famous?

✓ YES   ____NO

9. Is this your passion or someone else's?

✓ Mine   ____Someone else's

If you have answered yes to one or more of questions 1 through 8, then this journey is for you! If you have answered "someone else's" on #9 then you should take some time to consider going on this adventure because it's a big commitment of time and energy.

PARENT OR GUARDIAN QUESTIONS:

1. Do people stop you all the time and tell you how funny/beautiful/talented your child or teenager is?

___YES   ___NO

2. Does your kid keep bugging you that he/she wants to be on TV?

___YES   ___NO

3. Is your child or teenager always singing/dancing for you or others?

___YES   ___NO

4. Is your child or teenager always performing for you and the family?

___YES   ___NO

5. Is your child or teenager always talking about what he/she is going to buy you when he/she becomes a star?

___YES   ___NO

6. Is your child or teenager watching TV or films and saying, "I can do that"?

___YES   ___NO

7. Is your child or teenager always imitating voices and people from movies and television?

___YES   ___NO

8. Does your child or teen see themselves as famous?

___YES   ___NO

9. Is this your child's or teen's passion or is it yours?

___CHILD'S   ___MINE   ___BOTH

If you answered yes to several of the questions above, this book can be very helpful in guiding a child's career. However, if your answer to question 9 is "MINE", don't take this journey because it will surely lead to disappointment and heartbreak for you and the child.

Too often in my many years of casting, I have witnessed families that have invested much time and money only to have the child finally sitting in an anticipated audition announce he doesn't want to do this, and that he hates acting and you for making him do it.

Believe me when I tell you that this situation will create much antagonism and unhappiness between the two of you, and that there will not be a successful outcome.

BUT if you did answer yes to one or more of questions 1 through 8 and your answer to question 9 is "CHILD'S" or "BOTH", then welcome aboard!

In the following chapters, I'll be talking to you, the aspiring actor. However, if your parent or guardian is actively engaged in helping your career, they should read it also. This way everybody will be on the same page ☺.

Chapter

2

YOU'VE DECIDED THIS IS FOR YOU

You are about to start a wonderful adventure. This is a step-by-step guide to achieving success as a young actor. If you are not currently active in some activity like Community Theater, acting , improvisation (also known as improv), singing, and/or dancing classes, workshops, school acting classes or even putting something up on the internet, this is what you need to do in order to get started.

Getting active in one or more of these activities is the next step.

Community Theater:

I have found with all of the thousands of young actors I have read over the years, that the kids who stand out the most are usually doing some sort of Community Theater, acting class or even taking a private class with a teacher.

Whether it's a **scene study**, **improvisation**, or even a **cold reading** class, they are putting in the time to learn this craft and have tools at their fingertips to use when auditioning or in their performances. All of these activities help to develop one's confidence and talent.

[**Scene study** is a class where students take scenes from a play or movie and present them to a teacher. **Improvisation** is a form of acting where one invents, composes or performs with little or no preparation. A **cold reading** is a reading-aloud from a script or from scenes without any rehearsal, practice or study in advance.]

Your local Community Theater is a great starting place for a career in acting. There are many shows that have young actors in the cast. This is an excellent learning ground because you have to go through the auditioning and rehearsal process and the experience of doing live shows. One of the many positive things about doing live theater is that it teaches you how to be part of a group. Performing live gives you the experience of being in the moment, because if something goes wrong, you have to think on your feet. Also, these performances are often attended by people seeking new talent, such as an Agent, Casting Director, Producer, etc.

To show you how important a group can be for an actor, I remember one particular talent that I noticed, who then became quite popular:

When he first started out, **Wayne Brady** was performing in Community Theater and with an improvisation troupe in Orlando, Florida. I met him while he was doing improvisation with a group for a show in Los Angeles. He was so funny and talented and had amazing timing. I made a point of seeing him after the show and suggested that he move out to Los Angeles, which he did! He took those talents and eventually became part of a show called, *Whose Line Is It Anyway?* which was all about improvisational skills and quick wit. He later went on to win a Primetime Emmy award for his performance in this show.

You might naturally have these talents and timing. Some kids actually do! You might make your parents and friends laugh hysterically and bring them to their knees. But this doesn't necessarily translate when you need to display that same charm and humor to a room full of Casting Directors, Producers and Directors who you don't know.

I have seen many young actors who have some raw talent, but don't quite know how to make their character or dialogue seem real and believable to the audience. If it is a comedy, they don't always understand comedic timing and if it is a drama, they don't know how to convey the dramatic moments in the scene. This is where a class or acting coach could be of benefit.

Acting Classes:

The best thing about being in a class or part of a theater group, is that it is a place to learn, practice, and find out what your strengths are. It also gives you the ability to try new things that you might not be comfortable with, like playing different kinds of characters, or being in situations not normally in your life. When you are in a class or theater group, you may also be with people who have been acting for a while.

This environment gives one the opportunity to learn from others. It should be a place where you feel that you can explore your talents and take risks. Not every class is the right class for every person, so it is up to you to find the one that fits best.

Is This The Class For You?

Everyone starts somewhere. You might feel afraid to try something new—but after being there awhile if you still feel this way, this is not the right class! You want to be in a class or part of a group with a teacher or director that you trust and feel comfortable with exploring your talents and trying new things. A friend of mine was in an acting class with **Tom Selleck** who started out in commercials, as the Marlboro Man (big, tall, rugged, handsome, cowboy-type). He wanted to play character parts but didn't know where his real strength was or that he could be funny. He discovered his talents by being in class and went on to have a huge career in drama and comedy.

Ryan Potter, who stars in the series *Supah Ninjas,* was in a martial arts class. He was an expert martial artist at the age of fourteen. When we were casting the pilot, we searched across the country in acting classes, schools and martial arts classes because the lead had to be great with martial arts. Ryan got the notice and came to an audition at our office. He had a definite talent which needed to be directed, so we sent him to an acting coach. His talent blossomed and he nailed the part. Now he is on a series, another dream come true!

Networking Opportunities At Classes:

Classes are also a great place to network, to find out who you can do a **showcase** with, find out who has an Agent, what other people are auditioning for, etc. It is also a good place to make friends and work together on scenes.

[An Acting **Showcase** is a group of actors who get together and perform scenes or monologues from movies, plays or original material for the purpose of displaying their talents in front of Agents, Managers, and Casting Directors in the hopes of furthering their careers.]

Many times the people you meet and work with in these classes become lifelong friends. You root for their success and likewise, they encourage you too. They can help with your shared goals. Acting is a group activity so you need other people to be in scenes and of course, if you do a play or musical or even a YouTube video, there will be many people involved in the project.

Build upon your strengths. If you are a good dancer or singer, enroll in dancing and singing classes. These will serve you well. These talents give actors confidence and are great for honing performance chops. **If you are funny and a good imitator, get into an improvisation class.** There are many faces to comedy including stand-up, so whatever area you are good at, continue to study and find groups to be part of. The more well-rounded you are, the better. If you can dance, sing, and act, these are all valuable talents to have.

Classes are meant to enhance and develop your talent. It is great to see kids and adults in classes working on their craft. You see people improve so much. It is fantastic to have the admiration of your teachers and peers, and the confidence you can gain from being in a class and knowing your skills.

Here's an interview with a talented up and coming young actress and singer, **Sabrina Carpenter**, who will be starring in a new Disney Channel series, *Girl Meets World*. Sabrina and her mother, Beth, have been navigating the Los Angeles and New York acting scene for a couple of years and have some great advice for you.

Lisa London: Sabrina, where did you grow up?

Sabrina Carpenter: In Allentown, Pennsylvania. We have a house there and my Dad and my older sister still live there, but we're working on moving to California.

LL: What made you decide that you wanted to become an actor?

SC: I started singing and dancing when I was just two years old and when I was six, I started taking lessons. I took tap, ballet, hip-hop modern, and jazz. I love dancing, but I never thought I could make my whole career out of dance. I continue with dance because I know my training will be so valuable to me as a singer and actress.

When I was ten years old I came out to California to see what acting was really about. I was taking workshops in Los Angeles—one every summer. My aunt, **Nancy Cartwright**, (she is the voice of Bart Simpson), set up some meetings with Agents, Managers, and Casting Directors. I wasn't really able to sign with representation at that time because we were still living in Pennsylvania and we weren't ready to commit to coming out to L.A. yet.

LL: How did you get a manager?

SC: From the meetings I had while I was in Los Angeles, I had gotten several agent's business cards and Darci Price's was one of them, but she was now a manager with Bill Perlman at Perlman Management Group. When I was ready to get representation, we called Darci and I sang for her, did a scene, and she really believed in me. Then she set up a meeting for me with Bill Perlman in New York. We met with Bill, talked for three hours, and by the time we left, I had representation with Bill and Darci at Perlman Management Group.

We started doing video auditions from the East coast for L.A., and they would send me to local auditions in New York. The more and more auditions I did, the better I got. I auditioned for a guest star role on *Law & Order: Special Victims Unit* and I booked my first job. It was a day shoot in New York City, and I had a scene with **Christopher Meloni.** It was very serious, and scary. When I did this I thought, I can do this!

Beth Carpenter: Eventually we came out to California the following year for the end of pilot season. I was still working full-time and it was the only time I could get away from my practice—two weeks at the end of March. Sabrina got to go out on a few auditions and got a couple of callbacks. We went back home and Sabrina continued to do video auditions as well as commute to NYC for local opportunities. She did an audition on tape for American Girl, and they had interest in seeing her for a Producer's' session and Mix and Match. While out here, she got a callback for a Disney pilot that she initially auditioned for, was offered a screen test, and she booked it. If we hadn't come out for the American Girl audition, we would not have been here for the Disney pilot callback that led to a booking. [In a **Mix and Match** session, the top choices for the roles are paired up and read together to see who fits the parts best.]

LL: Did you know that you always wanted to sing and dance? How did you know this was your passion?

~ Connections

SC: It was kind of all around me. My mom used to be a dancer, my dad was in a rock band and my sisters started dancing so I just kind of followed the Carpenter girls' dancing.

I started vocal lessons with my Mom's old teacher when I was six. Then I started working with a man, Didier Auger—he's French and I've never actually met him in person. It was all on e-mail. He gave me a specific song to learn. I filmed myself singing and sent it to him. He would send me an e-mail telling me what to change and what he felt I was doing right.

BC: He taught her how to breathe and gave her specific exercises that were operatic and improved her range tremendously. She practiced every single day. I knew she had this voice from the time she was very young, but people don't know what goes on behind the scenes, the hard work and dedication that is required and the commitment to it. It's a lot!

LL: How did you become a finalist on the Miley Cyrus contest?

SC: It was a singing contest on her fan site, Mileyworld.com. When I joined that fan site, I was nine. She was my first inspiration. When I saw *Hannah Montana*, that's when I knew I wanted to do singing and acting. I wanted to be famous, like her—I just didn't know all the hard work that came with it.

I submitted a video of me singing, *I Ain't in Checotah Anymore*, by **Carrie Underwood**. My dad videotaped me and there were over 10,000 entries. The initial group was chosen by Miley World and we got notification that I had made the cut and was in the top fifty. Then it went down to 40, 30, 20 and 10. On every elimination round, they would have us do a new video. I sang many different artists' songs.

My dad learned to love editing while making the videos and I learned a lot more variety of songs. It was supposed to be a two month contest and it went on for about a year. Because of the contest, I got to meet **Miley Cyrus** at her concert. I came in 3rd place against a fifteen and sixteen year old and I was ten at the time. So I got my start on YouTube.

BC: It was from the contest that we started getting calls from record producers who were interested in meeting with her. My husband and I realized that we needed to start moving forward because things were starting to happen fast.

That is when I remembered that we had met Darci Price back in Los Angeles. Her card fell out of a folder when we were planning to go meet a record producer in New York City. I called her and we told her what we'd been doing, she remembered Sabrina and was passionate about her, so she arranged a meeting with Bill Perlman for us while we were in New York City.

LL: When did you think it was the right time to come out to L.A.?

SC: It was sort of a natural progression. Last year, for pilot season, we came out to Los Angeles for six weeks. Luckily, we had family who put us up and gave us a car. I couldn't have done it without them. It was really my first pilot season. I went on a lot of auditions and screen tested for four pilots. I booked two pilots. One was in front of a live studio audience which was **multi-camera** and the other was **single camera**. One was picked up and I was a recurring guest star on it: *The Goodwin Games.*

> [**Multi-Camera** shows are usually filmed in front of a live audience with several cameras. **Single camera** shows are usually filmed without an audience and using only one camera.]

Then I booked a movie called *Horns* starring **Daniel Radcliff** and **Juno Temple**. I booked that off a tape when I was in Pennsylvania. For people who say you can't book off of a tape, it is possible, if you are right for the role. They flew us out to Vancouver to film it. I went back and forth between Vancouver and Los Angeles because I was still filming the *The Goodwin Games* at the same time.

Then I got the audition for the Disney pilot, *Girl Meets World*. I auditioned and got a callback. I met with the Producer, who had created *Boy Meets World*. I sang for them at the callback and they loved it. I screen tested with seven other girls. Then the Producers and network looked at younger girls for the role. But I wanted this show so badly, I never gave up on my dream. A few weeks later I got another callback and the Producer asked me to change my wardrobe a bit before the next screen test, so it was more jeans, punk style. The next morning when I came in for the screen test, I was wearing a concert T-shirt, a leather jacket, ripped jeans and black boots.

We were reading with different girls and the Producer had me spend some time bonding with the actress I would play opposite. We talked and found out that we loved the same music and had lots of things in common. This gave us more of a relationship when we went in and auditioned together. Eventually she and I got cast as the lead roles of Riley and Mya and I was so excited.

LL: How do you feel about auditioning?

SC: Some are easier than others. I look forward to getting a new script and working on it. It's always great to meet a new Director and Casting Director, because even if I don't get it, it's another person that knows you.

LL: Did you have any trouble navigating the Hollywood scene?

BC: Not too much. **Nancy Cartwright** and our Managers were very helpful in pointing us in the right direction as far as turning us onto teachers and getting headshots. There's a lot of networking within the industry itself. I did get her into some classes. We've been really lucky; we've met so many wonderful people. We congratulate people when they achieve success. Sabrina has friends who she has met at auditions because a lot of times you see the same girls.

SC: There are some actors that are very competitive, but don't get me wrong I'm competitive too, but you are not always going to be right for every single role. You have to accept that and support the other girls who get it. You're all in a callback or screen test for a particular reason.

LL: Did you have a particular goal that you made early in your career?

SC: To win an Oscar, still working on that—laughs.

LL: Any actors or actresses who are influential to you?

SC: Definitely when I started working—**Miley Cyrus**. I love her for all the achievements she's made. I love **Jennifer Lawrence** for winning an Academy Award at such a young age. Not just for that, but for her acting techniques which are flawlessly real and relatable. Also, I love **Emma Stone**.

LL: What advice would you give someone starting out who does not live in LA?

SC: I would definitely say, it's possible—anything's possible as long as you have a support system around you. If your parents support you, then don't let anything stop you. But definitely work on your technique and perfect your craft.

BC: I would say get involved in the market closest to you, try to get connected there. Commercials come out of New York, Florida, Los Angeles, Chicago—Dallas is a huge market—and Atlanta. There are definitely places that people can somehow logistically get connected to. Every time Sabrina came out to LA, things really happened. I definitely feel that LA is the Mecca of the industry. If you can get out here for a pilot season, I really think that is #1, even if you don't book anything, just for the experience of it.

LL: What is the best advice you received?

BC: The best advice I got is for me to prepare and educate myself and learn the market. Not to give up, because as soon as you think one door has closed another door opens up. It's a numbers game; you walk into a commercial audition and a couple minutes later you walk out, it just means you're one step closer.

LL: Any other advice you would give to someone else just starting out?

SC: If you really love it, do it and don't let anything stop you.

WORKBOOK PAGE

Use Google, Bing or other internet search engines to find acting classes for children or teens in your city or region. Your search terms can include "Improvisation Classes" and "Commercial On-Camera Classes" as well as phrases like "Acting for Teens" and "Community Theater".

Network with other parents and teachers for recommendations of classes, groups or summer camps for young actors. Ideally, these groups would be putting up dramas, comedies or musicals as part of the learning experience.

HEADSHOTS

Now that you are studying and really starting to understand your talent—you'll want to start auditioning soon. First things first, you need a headshot.

HOW TO GET A GREAT HEADSHOT AND WHAT MAKES IT A GOOD ONE.

A headshot is a photograph of your face and it is your calling card within every aspect of the entertainment industry.

These are the important things to know when getting a headshot taken.

You want to make sure the headshot really looks like you:

We are looking for your personality to come across in the picture. We've all heard the proverb, "The eyes are the window to the soul". Well, the most important part of a headshot is your eyes; they should look bright and compelling, they should "pop". By that I mean, when I look at your headshot, I want to get a real feel for who you are.

For example: Are you more serious? Do you have a twinkle in your eye? Are you mischievous, or are you sassy? Do you have a certain attitude? These are some of the things we notice in a headshot. If you appear bored or have dull eyes, it won't be appealing. What do you want to communicate in your headshot? It's your personality! Remember that when taking your headshot, we want you to look your best, but as natural as possible. Don't try and look like somebody else.

What you wear is important:

Another important part of taking a headshot is what you wear. What makes your eyes "pop" or stand out? Are you wearing clothes that distract from your face? Are you wearing clothes that enhance your eyes, hair, and skin tone?

All headshots are done in color and you can take advantage of this opportunity by wearing a great color shirt or dress that makes your eyes stand out. Pick colors that will compliment your face.

Your headshots should mostly be close up shots; you can take a few ¾ body shots in case you need some for commercials and print. ¾ body shots usually include the body from just below the waist to the top of your head. Most headshots are taken from the chest up. Some people take them a bit below the chest, but remember, most submissions are done online so we really want to see those eyes and your face, even if we're looking at a small, thumbnail image on screen.

A few things to avoid when taking pictures:

- Busy backgrounds; lights that are too bright, or anything in the background that could be distracting from the main focus of the picture which is your face.

- Colors in the background that blend together too much with your skin tones.

- Clothes that are too busy such as plaid or paisley shirts.

- Shirts with words/logos/emblems.

- White shirts which tend to wash people out and can also be too reflective, depending on your skin tone.

- Backgrounds that are too dark.

- Keep your hands away from your face.

- Too much make-up, especially if you are a teenager.

- Excessive jewelry. In fact, less is more.

- Hair covering your eyes. It looks like you are hiding which is not going to help get you cast.

- If you are a young teenage girl **under** seventeen, don't take pictures showing cleavage. It sends the wrong message. Especially when you are trying to get cast on shows on the Disney Channel or Nickelodeon, or any time you're playing a young girl.

- Be aware; if while taking the pictures you need to squint due to the sun shining in your eyes, or you have any feeling of discomfort in the shoot, tell your photographer right away. Don't wait till the shoot is over.

- The more natural you look the better!

HERE ARE SOME EXAMPLES OF DIFFERENT TYPES OF HEADSHOTS:

The headshots presented on the following pages are printed in black & white. In order to see them in color, please go to the corresponding website for this book, **www.fromstarttostardom.com.** You will need a password to view the color headshot examples. That password is: **start2stardom**. All lower case, no spaces or quote marks.

Take a look at these headshots. Before you turn the page to see my comments about each one, see if you can identify what the subtle and not so subtle differences are in each group of pictures. Decide which ones you like the best? Then go to the next page and see what I think.

Actor: Collin Levin

Headshot A: The hat is distracting and makes his forehead prominent.

Headshot B: This would be a good headshot, but when you look at it in color on our website, there is a distracting red line behind him

Headshot C: This is a good headshot.

Headshot D: This could be a good headshot but ultimately the picture is all about his shirt.

Actor: Cassie Brennan

Headshot A: Not a good hairdo, face looks washed out and expression looks forced, not natural.

Headshot B: Bad angle for a headshot.

Headshot C: Scarf and headband and hand are distracting, all take away from her face.

Headshot D: This is a good headshot.

Actor: Kaden Hetherington

Headshot A: The design on his shirt is distracting from his face.

Headshot B: This is a good headshot.

Headshot C: The plant in the background is where your eyes go and you can't see his face well.

Headshot D: I don't normally recommend wearing plaids for your headshot, but in this instance, the colors in his shirt bring out his eyes nicely. Look at this headshot in color on our website to see what I mean.

Actor: Meg DeLacy

<u>Headshot A</u>: Good shot overall, but the shirt is distracting and takes away from her face.

<u>Headshot B:</u> This is too suggestive and inappropriate for her age.

<u>Headshot C:</u> This is good headshot.

<u>Headshot D:</u> Awkward cropping, off center, trying to be too artistic for a headshot.

Actor: Juliocesar Chavez

Headshot A: Goofy expression.

Headshot B: This would be a good headshot, but the striped shirt takes away from his face.

Headshot C: The background is distracting due to the yellow lights behind him. See for yourself on our website.

Headshot D: This is a good headshot. I normally don't suggest wearing white in a headshot, but with his skin color, this works nicely.

Theatrical and Commercial Headshots:

You want a theatrical and commercial shot. Theatrical headshots are <u>usually non-smiling</u> and more natural looking and commercials shots are usually smiling and more animated. When you go out for a commercial, you are auditioning to help the company sell a product. You usually want to appear animated and enthusiastic. You want your photo to reflect what you really look like.

Under 18? Look Your Age:

If you are under eighteen years old, your headshot needs to reflect your actual age. For example, if you are a thirteen or fourteen year old girl, look like that in your picture. Don't try and look seventeen. Knock off the heavy makeup. It will make you look older. Even if you think you look "so much better with the makeup," don't do it! Less is more, I promise you. Leave it to the professionals—it's always easier to add makeup than to expect the Casting Director or Producers to imagine what you would look like with less. This can make a dramatic difference to your look.

Look Like Your Headshot:

If you change your hair color and were a brunette and are now a redhead, you need to shoot new headshots. If you have gained or lost a lot of weight, then you need to re-shoot new photos. If your headshots are more than a year old, have new ones taken because your pictures should portray your current image.

As a Casting Director, when we pick you to come in and read, we go by your headshot. If you come in to a casting session and don't look similar to your headshot, then that is frustrating for us; especially if we're going for a certain look. For example, we have a part to fill that is a son of a mom or dad, and the Producer's want the kid to be blond, if you were a blond in your picture and then come in and are a brunette, that would be a problem. It can be difficult to get in and see certain Casting Directors, especially when you are just starting out. You don't want to blow it by coming in looking completely different than your headshot. Always put your best foot forward and look like your picture.

Before you make big plans for your photo shoot, really think about what your best look is going to be. If you've been dying to change your hair color or cut your bangs—go do it! And then really evaluate—does this look better than your original color or were you better off in the first place? If you are waiting to get that great haircut, do it before you shoot your photos.

Finding a Photographer:

You need professional headshots, and for that you need an experienced photographer. How do you go about finding one? Research. Go online, explore photographer's websites and see if you like their shots and if their price works for you. If you like the pictures your friends have, find out who took their headshots. Prices can range from $150 to $500 or more for a few different looks.

Some of you may have a friend or family member that takes great photos. This can present problems, unless they are professional photographers. It can become a sticky situation if they take photos and you don't like them. You might have to reshoot. Even if a person is a professional, but doesn't specialize in headshots, you can end up not getting the best pictures.

Once you have found two or three professional photographers, call them and talk to them. These are some of the questions you can ask them:

- How much do they cost?

- How many different looks and outfit changes for that amount of money?

- Does it include a DVD or access to a website with all the shots?

- How many of the shots will the photographer retouch?

It is most important that you feel comfortable with the photographer you select so that you can communicate with him or her and get the best headshots for yourself, child, teenager or young adult.

What do I look for in a headshot? I am looking for your personality to come across in the picture. Is there that sparkle that is going to make me want to click the button and look at your resume? Is your headshot going to make me want to bring you in to read? What are you trying to represent in the picture?

Retouching:

You should always get your picture retouched if there are any funny lines or marks or dark circles under the eyes, etc. Retouching can be done by the photographers or by the place where you get the pictures printed. It is up to you who does the retouching. It's usually just a matter of cost. You want your pictures to look the best, but you don't want them retouched to the point that you look airbrushed.

Thumbnails: —that's annoying

A thumbnail is an image that's been reduced in size so that many such images could be displayed on one computer screen or web page. Most headshots are first viewed as thumbnails on a computer screen by Industry professionals. If something about that thumbnail intrigues me, I will click on it to view a larger version of the headshot, the actor's resume and other photos he or she has online. It's important that you choose headshots that still manage to exude personality and spark when viewed as a one inch thumbnail image.

Most submissions for casting are done online and through the internet so you want to make sure that your picture "pops". When you are searching for an Agent and Manager, you will send them a printed headshot and/or a digital picture and resume via email.

Choosing Your Headshot:

In addition to digital versions of your headshots, you will also need a supply of hard copy, printed photos. These are my thoughts on how to decide which headshots to print. You need to go through the pictures and pick the ones you like. If you happen to have an Agent, Manager or a friend in the business, have them pick out their favorites. It's possible you could end up with ten to twenty-five different images that you or your team think are the best.

Then go to the local drugstore and print 4 x 6's of the favorite pictures. Your next step is to take those 4 x 6's and ask at least **ten** people (not just your family) their opinion of which one they like the best. You will see that probably two or three quickly become the "selects" and those are the ones to use.

Sometimes an Agent or Manager will pick something different than the pictures you like. Listen to them, they are professionals! I always tell actors, if the Agent wants to use that shot and it works to get you auditions, then don't change it.

Once you've selected your headshots, you want to print about fifty pictures to start; twenty-five commercial and twenty-five theatrical headshots. On these printed headshots, make sure that your name is printed on the bottom front of the picture. Whether you put your name in the middle or the side and the typesetting, is up to you. The reason for this is that if your picture and resume get separated, we will still know who you are. Some agents only want your name on your resume but this is a personal choice.

Postcards: ~ that's a lot

Once you have picked your headshots, you can also use them to make postcards. These can be used as a thank-you note after an audition, or to let industry professionals know that you are in a show, a movie, a commercial, or a play. They can also be used to let people know that you have new representation or have an upcoming showcase you would like them to attend. They are a great marketing tool. Always be sure to have your contact information on the card so they can reach you or your representation easily.

Always bring your headshots to the audition:

Even though we select the pictures online of the actors we would like to see, when you come to the audition, we collect the pictures and keep them in a file for our callbacks and future projects. Our Producers and Directors like to look at the hard copies of the pictures and resumes during the casting sessions.

When you go for a commercial, the headshots and resumes aren't always collected, but **you should always bring them to all auditions as a matter of habit.** I cannot stress this enough. This is also a sign of a professional.

Interview with Brad Buckman:

A favorite in Hollywood, top actor headshot photographer **Brad Buckman** is referred by leading Agents, Managers, Coaches, and Casting Directors. We have interviewed Brad to give you an even greater in-depth look at how to prepare for your photo shoot and how to pick your photographer:

Lisa London: We've been talking to our actors about some "don'ts" regarding headshots. Can you talk about what actors can do to get the best possible pictures?

Brad Buckman: Almost all actors feel some anxiety about getting headshots, whether they're new to the business or have been working for years, so there is good news and bad news. The good news is that you are not alone; everyone gets stressed about new pictures. The bad news is that you will always feel nervous about your upcoming session, but that's okay.

Headshot sessions have a lot in common with auditions. Auditioning is not your favorite thing to do either, but it is also a key step in the casting process. Your goal is to embrace and take control of both your auditions and headshot sessions, and make them work for you. They are both opportunities to perform and express yourself, so have fun!

LL: Where does an actor start?

BB: Actors are often frustrated by the lack of control they have over their careers. It is true that you are waiting to be chosen for auditions, callbacks, and jobs, but there is a lot you can do to increase the chance of those things happening. First, and most importantly, understand who you are as an actor. This knowledge will drive the rest of the decisions you make regarding your photographs, including what to wear, how to style your hair, whether to shave, and what to express in your face, eyes, and body language.

You have to make the distinction between who you are in real life, and who you are as an actor. You may be a very nice person, but your casting could be for darker characters. Your casting type may evolve over time, and can even change significantly. If you are new to the business, you can start with some very simple questions. First, consider the age range you will play. Some people appear to be much younger than their actual age, while others always appear to be more mature. One actor may have a narrow range, while another may cover a wide range as they vary their wardrobe, hairstyle, and attitude. Next, think about whether you'll be perceived as the sweet girl, or the bad girl, the nice guy, the jerk, or the one we're not quite sure about. Start thinking in broad strokes, and then you can begin to get more specific about the characters you're likely to play.

LL: What should an actor wear?

BB: There are several things to think about regarding wardrobe: style, color, texture, fit. Choose clothes that fit well and make you feel good. I prefer rich colors over bright colors. You often hear people talk about jewel tones, like a rich sapphire blue, emerald green, ruby red, etc. These can help to create a beautiful photo. Wearing a top that matches your eye color can be very striking.

It's best to keep the clothes simple, minimizing any prints, patterns, stripes, and logos. A key feature to consider is the neckline, and how it serves to frame your face. I encourage actors to take close-up snapshots in the outfits they are considering to see how they work in a photo. You can do this with clothes in your closet, as well as while you are out shopping.

Along with clothing, you'll want to carefully consider your hair color, cut, length, and style. These seemingly simple choices can greatly affect your casting, and these decisions will come out of your process for determining your type. Brown hair, red hair, blond, dirty blond, platinum blond. Long hair, short hair, spikey hair, bangs.

Men also need to consider if facial hair contributes to the look they are after. Beards are best avoided, but that scruffy look has been popular for a number of years in film, TV, and commercials. Often we'll shoot a look or two with the scruff, then shave for a cleaner look. There's no single right way to go, just what works for your type.

LL: Do you recommend hair and makeup services for your clients?

BB: I absolutely recommend that women take advantage of professional hair and makeup services. For actor headshots, the same artist will typically do both hair and makeup. The goal with the makeup is a clean and natural look, but this is not to be confused with wearing little or no makeup. We're doing makeup specifically for still photography, and the makeup artist is taking into account where you are shooting, the lighting, the camera, etc. Women should come with their face clean (just moisturizer), and their hair done the way they typically wear it. The makeup artist will help to style the hair, but you want to stop short of having the hair over-done, with a fancy blow out for example.

For men, makeup is more of a personal thing, and we refer to it as "makeup and grooming." Some experienced actors are used to wearing makeup when they perform, so they hire a makeup artist for the session.

Others are uncomfortable wearing makeup and go without. We provide translucent powder in that case, to minimize shine on the actor's face. I recommend that male actors have a basic makeup kit for auditions, performances, and photo shoots. They can go to any cosmetics store and get help with specific products that are right for them, and instruction on how to apply them. In the end, we want to keep everything clean and natural, and men should never look like they are wearing makeup.

LL: How should the actor prepare mentally?

BB: The frustrating thing about photo shoots for actors is that they are not about acting. Actors are thrilled to be on stage or on set, ready to inhabit a character and interact with the other performers. But ask them to get some photos of them being themselves, and they break into a cold sweat. A client walked in for her session one day, telling me how much she hates getting her pictures done. I told her it makes me feel like a dentist, and she laughed, saying, "I was just on the phone with my girlfriend saying I'd rather be going to the dentist right now."

We've been talking about external factors like wardrobe and makeup, but it is just as important to consider an actor's mental preparation. On the one extreme, many actors come in and say, "I like your pictures, let's shoot." I work to help them relax, and we casually converse and take pictures. On the other end, an actor might come with prepared monologues, or individual bits of dialog they want to say while we're shooting.

It's important to look for characters that you might portray in movies, TV shows and commercials. Study those performances, see how the actors express themselves, note their hairstyles and wardrobe. You can treat your photo session as more of an acting exercise, and channel a character's energy, internalize their emotions. It may be as simple as choosing a word to focus on while shooting, or more actively delivering individual lines, or even reciting a monologue.

Whatever helps the actor to express themselves is fine with me. I also recommend that performers think about the music we'll play during the session. We have access to just about everything, but often clients will create their own playlists for the shoot, going as far as pulling songs for each emotion they want to express.

LL: How should actors choose a photographer?

BB: What they should NOT do is simply shop by price. Many actors call around and ask, "How much does it cost?" Your headshots play a vital role in your career, and you need to take them seriously. The entire process can get expensive, but it's worth the investment to get pictures that get you in the room. Once you have photos that really work, you understand just how important they are, and the difference they can make.

Ask around to find out which photographers other actors have used recently. Ask about their experience, as well as the final photos. You can also search the web for photographers in your area, and review their websites.

Look for a consistency in the photography, and see if they have a style that you like. Pretty pictures are nice, but do you want to meet the people you see? Do they seem relaxed, and do you feel you really have a sense of the person who will walk into the room? Is there a focus on the face and the eyes? Is the expression genuine?

It's nice if you can meet the photographer in advance, to see where they work, talk about their approach, and see if you feel a connection. Finding someone who can help you through the process is key, and you need to know that they truly care about your success.

WORKBOOK PAGE

Exercise 1: Go through your closet and pick out a couple of outfits to be photographed in.

Exercise 2: Take a picture of yourself on your smart phone—does the outfit make your eyes "pop"? Continue this exercise until you've identified colors and/or tops that accentuate your eyes.

Exercise 3: Make a list of characters you ~~would like~~ to play or be cast as. *- type cast*

Character 1: the girl next door

Character 2: the fighter

Character 3: thee nerdier girl

Character 4:

Character 5:

Exercise 4: Go into your closet and find a shirt or piece of clothing that will help you get into the character(s) you've listed above.

RESUMES

Wikipedia defines resume as a document used by individuals to present their background and skill set. Resumes can be used for a variety of reasons but most often to secure new employment.

An actor's resume is a little different than that of a typical job seeker. It should list his or her physical characteristics (height, hair color, eye color) acting credits (projects he or she has done), contact information (usually the Agent or Manager), and skills (sports, languages, hobbies, etc.).

Let's get started making your resume.

First you need to make some lists of all the productions you have participated in, whether it be school plays, community theater, internet projects, web series, commercials, television projects, and films. Now, I realize that if you are just starting out, you probably won't have film or television projects yet on your resume and that is okay. Every actor starts somewhere.

Miley Cyrus, who I cast in the pilot of *Hannah Montana*, had no credits other than being on stage performing with her dad, **Billy Ray Cyrus**, and *Hannah* was her first theatrical gig.

So don't despair!!

When you are first starting out, any of these performances can be used on your resume:

- Singing or dancing at a recital

- Performing in a play at your school, church, or a performing arts center

- Participating in a on-line project or a student film for your school

- A performance in a workshop or a showcase

- Acting in a scene study, commercial, or improvisation class

Here are some ideas on how to build a resume even if you don't have a lot of credits. You can film a scene, do a monologue, sing a song, do a stand-up routine, make a music video, or make your own talk show and put it on YouTube. This is your moment to get creative and show off your talent.

You never know who will see it and want to meet you, such as an Agent or Manager, Casting Director, etc. It is also a way to start building credits on your resume.

Another way to build credits and get experience in front of the camera is to do commercials. Many people have started out acting in commercials and built up their resumes from there. For teens and kids, commercials are a good learning ground, both for being on set and in front of the camera, and becoming comfortable with auditions.

In this day and age, there is no shortage of ways to build credits since we are in such a technological age. One piece of advice— if you film something; make it look as professional as possible. You can film a scene indoors or outdoors, but make sure the location is up to professional standards. Use professional lighting (no shadows on faces unless it enhances the mood of the scene).

In film, a Long Shot is a view of a scene that is shot from a considerable distance. If the entire performance is filmed from a long shot, it makes it very difficult to actually see you perform. Remember to use close ups that will help show your emotions as an actor.

Greyson Chance is a singer who uploaded a video of himself singing onto YouTube. **Ellen DeGeneres** got wind of him and brought him on her show. Much of Chance's celebrity began with a fortuitous performance by the stage-ready 6th grader for his fellow students of Lady Gaga's, *Paparazzi*. The now infamous performance of *Paparazzi* in April 2010 went on to become YouTube's #3 most popular video of 2010 and has received nearly

45 million views to date. Catching the eye of a producer at *The Ellen DeGeneres Show*, led to Chance's first guest appearance and a fateful return a week later, where DeGeneres announced that she had signed Greyson as the first artist on her newly formed label, ElevenEleven.

How to make the resume:

Put your name at the top with your contact information. If you are lucky to have representation, put your agent or manager's number and name of their company. If you don't have representation then I suggest using your parent's name and phone number. If you are over eighteen, put your own number if you don't have representation yet.

Then you put your eye color and hair color. Some actors put date of birth and height on their resume when they are just starting out. **When you are over eighteen, never put your date of birth or age on your resume.** The reason is that if you look younger and can play younger, but you are over eighteen, stating your age destroys the illusion.

Here is an example of how that can work for you: When I auditioned **Jason Earles** for the role of Jackson, Hannah Montana's older brother, we were looking for someone who was sixteen years old. When Jason auditioned for me, I asked how old he was and he told me nineteen. I told him that when he came in to see the Producers, he needed to tell them he was seventeen. He looked like he was only sixteen or seventeen years old so it wasn't a huge stretch. I knew that if he said his real age he would most likely be ruled out because of it. When he came in for the callback, he said he was seventeen years old. He got the part! Later after the series was filming, I came to find out that Jason was quite a bit older than nineteen years old—he was playing me like I was playing the Producer. The Producers, Jason, and I all had a good laugh about it.

Part of the casting process is about perception. How old do you look and how young can you play?

The amount of hours a minor can work on the set are based on how old the actor is. It is less if you are under eighteen. Minors are not only limited to the amount of hours they can be on camera, but all minors have to continue their schooling, even on a set. It is a good thing if you look young but have the benefit of being eighteen or older—so use it.

The next part of the resume, after your name, contact info, eye color, hair color, height, and date of birth if you are under eighteen, is formatting the resume. This is how you go about doing this.

Divide your 8½ x 11 paper in three columns with no lines. The reason you use three columns is because it is easier to read compared to text in paragraph form. As Casting Directors, we glance at the resumes so you want them to be simple to read.

These are the different categories and they should be in this order:

- FILM

- TELEVISION

- (If no Television, you can have a category of COMMERCIALS)

- A Web-series or YouTube videos can be listed under television or you can have an INTERNET category on your resume

- THEATER

- TRAINING

- SPECIAL SKILLS

In the first column, whether it is a film, television, commercial, internet or theater project, list the title of the project that you were in under each heading. When starting out it is fine to list your commercial or music video credits.

In the second column, if it is a Film or Television project, list the size of the role that you played. For example if you were the lead in the feature, you list Lead. If you were the co-lead, supporting, co-star, featured, etc., that is what you say.

In Television, for example, you might have a co-star role, an under five role (which is five lines or under). In a commercial, you could be the lead or the main person in the commercial or in a YouTube Video, you might be the lead. It is better not to list the name of the role that you played because if we didn't see that television show or that movie, the name of the character isn't what matters. It is always the size of the role.

In theater, list the name of the play and the role you played. For example, you were Dorothy in *The Wizard of Oz*. The character name you played is what would go in column two. Live appearances can be listed under theater also. Let's say you were in a performance at school, you would list the title, what role you played, and where you performed it.

When you are first starting out, we don't expect that you played leads. It is okay to be part of the chorus, ensemble, etc. This is a way to round out your resume.

The third column for film and television would be listing the Director of the project, or the studio, production company, or the name of the network. Otherwise, you can put that it is an independent film, a student film, or that it was on YouTube.

For theater, always list the name of the theater where you performed.

On your training, list who you study with and whether it is scene study, improvisation, on-camera, private coaching, singing, dancing, etc.

On your special skills, list a few lines of the things that you CAN do, NOT the things that you wish you could do. If you can't play baseball then don't write it down. But if you can play some sports, list the ones you can play. Sometimes, we call actors in based on their special skills, so don't say you are a great horseback rider, if you have never been on a horse. Another example is, don't say you can tap dance if you only took one class or claim you can do gymnastics or rollerblading if you're not proficient at it. This is true especially if auditioning for a TV show because they move very fast and you can ruin some future opportunities if you say you have a skill when you don't. If you are up for a movie, sometimes they have more time to train you in the specific skill that the role calls for, but not always.

If you are a great hula hooper then you would list that under special skills. If you have some interesting, fun special skill that you can do, put that down. One young lady put on her resume that she could do Betty Boop impressions and we asked her to perform them. Some special skills will open the door to be a topic of conversation when you are having an interview for an Agent, Manager, Casting Director, or Producer. It is always good to have a conversation-starter and one of your special skills could be just that.

Your resume is an ongoing, changing document because as you get more and more work, you will continue to update your resume and get pickier as to what credits to keep. If you get an acting gig as a regular on a television series, some of the first credits when starting out would probably come off. But never take an impressive credit off. For example, if you were in *West Side Story* at a community theater and played Tony, you wouldn't take that off your resume. The reason is that it shows a good theater credit, that you can carry the lead of a show and probably have a pretty good singing voice too!

<u>The one thing to never do is lie on a resume</u>. Don't put down you were in a show or a film that you weren't in. If a movie comes to your town to film and you weren't in it, don't put it down! I can tell you a number of stories where actors got caught lying about their credits by the Casting Directors who actually cast those projects.

On the following pages I provide examples of real actor resumes.

Cassie Brennan
SAG

Hair: Blonde Eyes: Blue Height: 5'1"

FILM:

Endgame	Starring	Dir: Carmen Marron
Single Mom's Club	Supporting	Dir: Tyler Perry
Alone Yet Not Alone	Supporting	Mission City Productions
Spring Forward	Starring	Dir. Zach Yokam
Clapham Project	Supporting	Dir. Aaron Steiner
April Showers	Supporting	Dir. Jordan Imhoff
The Rental	Supporting	Dir. Jake Wright
Water, Water Everywhere	Starring	Dir. Aaron Steiner
Cold Showers	Supporting	Dir. Andrea Murphy
Heaven Whispers	Starring	Dir. Jennifer Byrd
Push Came To Shove	Supporting	Shoestring Productions

TELEVISION:

Twisted	Recurring Co-Star	ABC Family
Wicked Attraction	Guest-Star/Jaycee Dugard	Discovery Channel
Wicked Attraction	Co-star	Discovery Channel

COMMERCIALS AND INDUSTRIALS: List Available Upon Request

THEATER:

Legally Blonde	Elle Woods	Kids On Broadway/Theatrix Productions
Hairspray	Chorus/Dancer	Kids On Broadway/Theatrix Productions
The Drowsy Chaperone	Chorus/Dancer	Kids on Broadway/Theatrix Productions
Kicks: The Showgirl Musical	Rockette	Kids On Broadway/Theatrix Productions
How to Succeed in Business w/o Really Trying	Chorus/Dancer	Kids On Broadway/Theatrix Productions
Seussical Jr.	Bird Girl	Regent University

VOICEOVER:

Bresnan Communications	Mary	Earworks
Democratic Party	Student	Earworks
Water, Water Everywhere	Child in Boat/Principal	Regent University

TRAINING:

Marnie Cooper	**Ongoing** Kids Acting Program and Coaching
Andrew Magerian	**Ongoing** Kids Acting Program
Millennium Dance Complex	**Ongoing** Dance and Voice Lessons

SPECIAL SKILLS:
Cries on Cue, Physical Comedy, Improv, Action/Stunt, Soprano, German and Southern Accent, Singing, Reading, Bicycling, Basketball, Running, Swimming, Creative Writing, All Animals, Reptiles, and Insects

CTG Young People's Department
Jody Alexander / Bonnie Ventis / Philip Marcus
Phone: 818-509-0314 / Fax: 818-509-7729 / 10950 Ventura Blvd, Studio City, CA 91604

COLLIN LEVIN

Hair: COPPER RED
Eyes: BROWN

FILMS:

Reality	Lead	Student Film
Not an Ordinary Guy	Co-Star	Dir. Jake Isham

TELEVISION:

Supah Ninjas	Co-star	Nickelodeon
Kirstie Alleys Big Life	Co-star	A&E
Arliss	Co-star	HBO

COMMERCIALS/PRINT:

Mazda	Lead	TYO Productions
Samsung Electronics	Lead	Duo Films

MUSIC VIDEO:

Crying	Lead Actor	Dir: Denice Duff
Can't Let Go	Lead Actor	Dir.: Kyle Jones

THEATRE:

Super Villain Comics	Drummer	Millikan Theatre
Tuesday Night Live	Actor, Singer, Dancer	Alex Theatre

TRAINING:

Acting	Acting Center	Amanda Rogers/Lee Burns
Improvisation	Acting Center	Tait Ruppert
Commercials	Acting Center	Eric Matheny
Commercial Workshop	Stephanie Lesh/Francine Selkirk	
Acting, Singing, Dancing	Summer Acting Camp	Justin Eick

SPECIAL SKILLS:
Amazing Drummer, Guitar, Piano, Baseball, Basketball, Soccer, Tennis,
Volleyball, Stage Combat, Skateboarder, Bicycling, Photographer

KADEN HETHERINGTON
SAG-AFTRA

EYES: BLUE   WEIGHT: 100
HAIR: BROWN   HEIGHT: 5'
D/O/B: 5/23/01

FILM:
Bullies	Lead	Short Independent Film
Wini + George	Party Goer	Short Film
Light	Co-Star	Short Student Film

TELEVISION:
Sean Saves The World	Recurring (Young Sean)	NBC
Happy Endings	Co-Star	ABC

COMMERCIAL:
List of commercials available upon request.

PRINT:
Starmaker Designs - Dance Catalogue

TRAINING:
Tap	Karen Hyland; Ray Hesselink
Acro	Hector Salazar
Ballet	Max Baud; Northeast Academy of Dance – Giuseppe Canale
Acting	Bo Kane, Loren Chadima, Ezra Weisz, Phil DeChamplain, Melissa Skoff
Competition Dance	(Tap/Acro/Jazz/Ballet) Miss Lore's School of Performing Arts
Hapkido	Grandmaster Ho Jin Song, Genessa Borden, John Moody

SPECIAL SKILLS
Swim, bike, roller blade, ice skate, skateboard, yo-yo, cooking, gymnastics, magic, Hapkido martial arts (brown belt), learning ukulele, very knowledgeable in Greek, Norse, and Egyptian Mythology, and Chemistry (can recite the Periodic Table of the Elements)

CTG Young People's Department
Jody Alexander / Bonnie Ventis / Philip Marcus
Phone: 818-509-0314 / Fax: 818-509-7729 / 10950 Ventura Blvd, Studio City, CA 91604

WORKSHEET PAGE: Create your resume
RESUME TEMPLATE: Use the template below as a guide to gathering the information for your resume.

Representation name & Telephone # (or parent's #)

YOUR NAME: _____

Date of Birth: _____(for under 18)

Eye color: _____ Hair Color: _____

Height: _____ Weight:_____

Film
(Name of the Project)   Size of the Role: Director or Studio

Television or Internet
(Name of the Project)   Size of the Role: Studio / or Network

Commercials
 Product Name (or list upon request)   Size of the Role: National/Local

Theater
(Name of the Play)   Character's Name   Where Performed (theater or school)

Training
Acting	Scene Study	Name of Teacher or Class
Improv	(Name of Teacher)	Name of the Class
Dance	Type (ex: Hip Hop)	Teacher or Studio
Singing		Name of Teacher
Stand Up comedy	Name of Teacher	Name of the Class

SPECIAL SKILLS: Put into 2-3 sentences listing your special skills—from sports abilities, musical instruments you can play, anything unique about you (ex: impersonations, whistling, etc.)

HOW TO GET DISCOVERED AND PROMOTE YOURSELF

There are many ways to get discovered. You could have a certain look that someone is searching for, a certain attitude, a personality that is unique or maybe you are just beautiful, super funny or incredibly talented. Maybe you get plucked out of the group to be asked to audition for a particular project or commercial, because you happen to be in the right place at the right time and before you know it, you are on your way to your dream. With that being said, most of us have to work a lot harder to get discovered.

Certainly, putting yourself in the right places and exposing yourself to Industry people who are looking for talent gives you a leg up. You have a lot to do with making your own opportunities and "Luck". As Thomas Jefferson, the Third president of the United States, has said,

"I find that the harder I work, the more luck I seem to have."

The best luck is the luck you make yourself. Be prepared, work hard and get lucky!!

Here are some interesting examples of actors and actresses making their own luck. You can find them, as we did, on the internet.

Dakota Fanning was born, in Conyers, Georgia, USA. Ever heard of Conyers, Georgia? Well, that is a far cry from Hollywood. But she got discovered there. How?

Dakota went to a playhouse near her home, where the children that attended put on a weekly play for their parents. The people running the playhouse noticed that Dakota stood out, and advised her parents to take her to an agency. They believed that she was extremely talented. The Fanning family was advised to spend six weeks in Los Angeles, a long way from their home in Georgia. In Los Angeles, Dakota managed to get her first job; starring in a national Tide commercial. She was chosen out of many other children. As we all know, she has gone on to do wonderful work.

Brad Pitt told his parents he intended to enroll in the Art Center College of Design in Pasadena, but instead spent the next several months driving a limousine—chauffeuring strippers from one bachelor party to the next, delivering refrigerators, and trying to break into the Los Angeles acting scene. He joined an acting class and, shortly after, accompanied a classmate as her scene partner on an audition with an agent. In a twist of fate, the agent signed Pitt instead of his classmate. After weathering only seven months in Los Angeles, Pitt had secured an agent and regular acting work.

Talk about a big break, there's no need to ask "How did **Emma Watson** get famous?" She landed the role of Hermione Granger in the *Harry Potter* films in 1999 and immediately became a household name. Though she was found through her acting teacher at the Oxford Theatre and producers were wowed by her natural talent, she still went through eight auditions before finally earning the part.

Mila Kunis' hometown was in the Ukraine until she was seven, at which time her family moved to Los Angeles. The move to a new country, with a new culture and new language, was a bit of a difficult transition for the young Kunis, as she learned English and tried to fit in with her peers. When she was nine, her parents enrolled her in a children's acting class in an attempt to help her make new friends. In this program, Kunis met Susan Curtis, the woman who would become, and still is, her manager.

New "It Girl", **Emma Stone**, now in her early twenties, discovered her acting skills at the age of eleven when she acted in her debut stage performance with Valley Youth Theatre. The young actress worked with the theatre which was near her home in Scottsdale, Arizona. At such a young age she was exposed to many talented actors and learned her basics of acting. *The Wind in the Willows* was her debut play as an actress after which she went ahead to play roles in more than a dozen plays at the theatre. She wanted to move to Los Angeles and prepared a PowerPoint presentation for her parents so that they would be convinced to send her to California and let her start her acting career. After moving to Los Angeles and going on many auditions, she got a break and was cast in a reality show, *In Search of The New Partridge Family*. I met Emma and gave her one of her first jobs when I was casting *The Suite Life of Zack and Cody* and could see that she was going to be a star. She did an episode of the show and we later cast her again as the lead opposite, **Anna Faris** in the movie, *House Bunny*.

Selena Gomez began her acting career when she was just seven years old by playing Gianna on a show called *Barney & Friends*. Selena was discovered by the Disney Channel in 2004 during their nationwide talent search. Her first Disney role was a series regular role on a pilot that I cast called, *What's Stevie Thinking?*, which did not get picked up for a series. But Disney loved her and kept looking for a project for her. We cast her in a guest appearance on *The Suite Life of Zack & Cody*. Then, in 2007 Gomez was cast as a series regular in the Disney series, *Wizards of Waverly Place*.

Taylor Lautner, in addition to his love for martial arts, quickly developed a love for acting at the age of seven years old. He had a martial arts instructor, who was involved in show business who encouraged him to audition for a small appearance in a Burger King commercial. Although he didn't get that commercial, he enjoyed the experience so much that he told his parents that he wanted to pursue an acting career. Soon, he and his family were traveling back-and-forth on a regular basis from their home in Michigan to California so Taylor could audition for acting roles.

When Taylor was ten, with the frequent traveling and air fares starting to become overwhelming, his family made the crucial decision to relocate to Los Angeles where Taylor would have the advantage of being able to audition for films, television, and commercials full-time. Once Taylor moved with his family to Los Angeles, he found himself landing more small acting roles. Smaller roles lead to bigger roles which lead to starring roles for this talented actor.

Born **Justin Randall Timberlake** on January 31, 1981, in Memphis, Tennessee. Timberlake grew up singing in the Baptist church choir. He began his career on *Star Search* and then was cast on *The Mickey Mouse Club*, starring with **Britney Spears** and **Christina Aguilera**. In 1995, he became a teen heartthrob with the pop group 'N Sync. The boy band would go on to become one of the hottest pop groups of the 1990s. From being a Grammy award winning musician, he continued to add to his resume as a successful career as an actor.

Here are some things you can do to start the ball rolling on your own career.

YOUTUBE:

Make a video and put it up on YouTube. You can make a music video, a monologue, an acting scene with another person, a stand-up routine, a funny interview, impressions, or any creative thing you can imagine that will show your talent. But make sure it is good quality and something you would be proud of other people seeing.

Also, if you make a video and put it on YouTube, you can add that as a credit on your resume. You don't need a ton of these on your resume, but when first starting out, a few of these credits are fine.

This has become so popular in finding new and young talent that Producers, Agents, Managers, Casting Directors and many others industry professionals spend their time combing the internet looking for talent.

One of the most successful new acts of 2012 that was found and developed from this avenue is **Sophia Grace** and **Rosie**. They are two little girls, ten year old Sophia Grace Brownlee and six year old Rosie McClelland who sang the **Nicki Minaj** song, *Super Bass*. Their parents thought the kids were so cute that they filmed them and then posted it on YouTube. It came to the attention of the people at *The Ellen DeGeneres Show*. They now have recurring roles on her show, and have books and merchandise deals with Walmart and K-mart, plus apps and games in their image. They have become an internet sensation and a marketing brand.

Lucas Cruikshank is a teenage director and actor who got his start by making videos with his cousins John and Katie, and posting them on YouTube. He came up with the character you all love, Fred, who is an annoying six year old with a dysfunctional family and is most noted for his sped-up voice. Lucas said that he created the first Fred video to poke fun at video bloggers who talk about every single thing that they're doing in the video. The first video received tons of positive feedback, and Lucas continued to post videos in the Fred series, which he edits, directs, and acts in by himself. Producer, Brian Robbins' sons saw the Fred videos and showed them to their dad. Brian thought he was very talented and ended up producing a movie, "Fred" which was later sold to Nickelodeon and then Lucas was cast in his first television series for Nickelodeon.

#1 youtube star!

SHOWCASES:

An Agent or Casting Director who is looking for talent comes to your city and you do a showcase.

A showcase is a small show put together by actors who present a scene, monologue, song or stand-up routine to an invited audience of entertainment people who can further their careers (i.e. Agents, Managers, Casting Directors, Producers, Directors, etc.) It is to showcase their talent and is a way to audition for many people at one time. It is also a chance to perform in front of an audience. Sometimes it is done through an acting class or a group of actors will put one together.

Everyone in the show makes a list of the people they know or have been in contact with that they could invite to the show. You will have to send them fliers and make calls to get people to come and see it. This will take some persistence on your part, and even if you can't get the Agents, Managers, or Casting Directors themselves to show up, get the assistants to come. You never know when today's assistant will be the next Agent, Manager, or Casting Director. Pictures and resumes are put together of all the participants and given out to the industry people who come to the show. These showcases can be as simple as an hour where one can see the showcase and have a bite, all on their lunch hour. Or it could be an evening performance, but each scene is usually no longer than two to five minutes long.

Whether it is a comedy or drama, pick a scene that shows your best work, and try to show your "castability". Don't pick a scene that calls for someone in their late twenties if you are in your teens! Pick something that is age appropriate. Scenes or monologues are taken from plays, TV shows, movies and some people even write their own. There are many monologue books for teens. Search online and find them. How elaborate you get with the showcase, is up to you or the acting teacher in charge of the class. But remember that you are there to show your best work so don't get complicated and make it all about the scenery, the make-up, or the special effects.

COMMUNITY THEATER:

Getting in a play and doing Community Theater is another way to also promote yourself. Make sure when you invite people to see the play, that it is a nice size role. You wouldn't want to invite people to see you if you only had a few lines, unless it's a "steal the scene" type character. It should be a significant part. Even doing plays in school is a good idea because it gives you experience and credits on your resume. And, you never know who in the entertainment business might show up in the audience. I have gone to a number of school plays that my own kids were in and saw talented kids I have brought in for auditions who had no representation.

Invite a local Agent or Manager to come see the show. Meet with them afterwards and set up a time to talk about your career. Hopefully you will hit it off and they will want to represent you.

Theater has many different forms and one can actually work in a professional stage situation but still be unknown to Television and Film Directors and Producers. Using the same promotional activities listed above can assist one in crossing over to other medias.

Megan Hilty was in the Broadway musical *Wicked,* and then joined the national touring company where I went to see her. She was so versatile and dynamic that we brought her in for a guest starring role and cast her in her first television show. Of course she has gone on to great success, starring in the television series, *Smash* and is currently on the show, *Sean Saves the World.*

ACTING CLASSES:

Acting classes are another way to not only improve your skills as an actor, but also it is a good networking place. A fellow actor in class might introduce you to their Agent or Manager. The acting teacher might possibly put on a showcase of all the actors in his or her class. The acting teacher could also have friends who are Casting Directors, Agents and Managers and invite them to sit in on a class or watch a showcase of the actors.

I have been invited to many acting classes where the teacher invited me to sit in and watch a showcase. I have found a number of talented actors and actresses this way. I remember one showcase where I saw this very talented girl; I brought her in for her first audition and she booked her first job on a series I was casting.

As a side note, I don't recommend doing showcases or acting classes that cost thousands of dollars. Sometimes, you will hear about things on the radio or advertised that are quite expensive. You can check them out. **But beware of promises to get you representation as part of their acting program.** Especially if you have to take a lot of classes and it includes taking photos of you, and costs thousands of dollars, I would be very cautious. It is possible that you might be seen by a legitimate Agent, Manager or Casting Director from one of these acting/modeling programs, but I do not feel that it is money well spent. There are many wonderful classes that don't cost a fortune that will be available to you. Remember, legitimate Agents and Managers don't get their commissions until you book a job, so there is no money upfront required.

GETTING AN INTERVIEW:

If you live in a smaller town that doesn't have a lot of industry people, but there is someone in a neighboring town that is working as an Agent or Manager, find a way to meet them. Besides sending your picture and resume with a short note, if that doesn't get you an interview, get clever. Maybe you bring them cookies along with your monologue. Don't be shy. Even if you only meet the assistant to that Agent at the moment, she could help by introducing you to her boss. Take every person you meet as an opportunity because you just never know where you might get discovered.

OPEN CALLS:

Sometimes, in your area you will read about an open call for a particular role in a movie, television show or play. If you fit the description, then I say, "Go For it" and get your butt out there and audition. Even if you don't get called back, it is worth the experience. But if you do get a callback then great, and even better, what if you get discovered?

There are many stories of people who went to an open call and got a lead in a National tour of a show or a part on a television show. I know one young man, **Kylend Hetherington**, who heard about the audition for "Billy Elliott" and went to audition for it, never having auditioned before and got the lead as Billy in the National tour. **You can see the interview about him and his auditioning process in Chapter 8.**

STUDENT FILMS: √

Another way to start building up credits on your resume is to act in a student film. The way you go about this is to contact your local colleges and universities and ask for the Film Department. Get an e-mail address and let them know you are an actor and would like to be notified when they are casting their films. Find out if you can send your picture and resume for their files, or what their filming procedures are. Sometimes even local high schools have a film department and need actors of all ages. If you get cast in one of these student films, make sure they agree upfront to give you a copy of the film, or at least a copy of your scenes.

OTHER AVENUES TO EXPLORE:

Many cities have a local film commission which is another way of finding who is going to be filming in your city or nearby town. Every city has a Chamber of Commerce and this is another bright idea of people to contact to find out what is filming in your area. Call and find out how to get on their mailing list so you can be notified when they are looking for local talent. This is a great way to start building up your resume!

ONLINE SUBMISSIONS:

You can submit yourself on certain websites such as:

- Actors Access: **www.actorsaccess.com**—this gives you access to all states. You just pick your region and sign up.

- LA Casting: **www.lacasting.com**—for projects casting in Los Angeles.

- San Francisco: **www.sfcasting.com**—for projects casting in the San Francisco area.

- Casting Networks: **www.castingnetworks.com**—for other states outside of California or other countries.

- Now Casting: **www.nowcasting.com**—for projects all over the country, just pick your primary location

- Casting Frontier: **www.castingfrontier.com**—just pick the region you live in.

- Cazt: **www.cazt.com**

- The People's Network: **www.thepeoplesnetwork.com**

Go to these web addresses, create an account and follow the directions on how to get started and set yourself up to be submitted. You will need to upload your pictures, plus fill in details about yourself including any special skills that you can do and create your resume.

Once you have an account set up and your picture and resume is online, go through the website and submit yourself for roles that are right for your age and look. Be advised, do not submit yourself for commercials in Los Angeles if you don't live in Southern California and cannot get to LA right away, because they cast and shoot very quickly.

These are all possible ways to build your resume and promote yourself. As you are working on getting an Agent and Manager when starting out, continue to build your resume and put yourself out there to experience new avenues of your career. It can be invaluable! Don't miss out on these opportunities because everyone starts somewhere. Even something that isn't the best experience can sometimes lead to meeting someone who can then help further your career or even make a friendship for life.

PERSERVERANCE is the key!!! There is no more important attribute that is greater than perseverance. Continuing to go for it, through any adversity or discouragement, is the key to success. As I said earlier in this chapter, **Be Prepared, Work Hard and Get Lucky!**

SAFETY POINT:

As a point of safety, I would recommend that you always take someone with you when going to meet an adult who has requested a meeting, especially if you are under eighteen years old. (This can include an Agent, Manager, Photographer, Producer, Director, Casting Director, etc.) This is just a piece of advice, not meant to scare you, but as a word of caution. There are people out there looking to take advantage of young talent and who pretend to be legitimate industry professionals, but they have other motives. It's always best to be aware and take someone along with you to these meetings and stay safe.

Here's an interview with **Jason Earles**, a successful young actor I cast as a series regular in *Hannah Montana*.

Lisa London: What made you decide that you wanted to be an actor? What age did you start?

JE: I think I was always interested in being an actor. The first play I was ever in was a third grade production of *Hansel and Gretel*. I was hooked. My mom would say I was an actor from the time I was very little, even before I knew what acting was. There are pictures of me at the age of four or five, sitting at the table next to a beer bottle pretending like I had a hangover. I was always acting silly to get extra attention.

LL: Did you do any kind of classes, improv, theater?

JE: I took every acting/theater class available from elementary school on. I loved to practice. I always felt like the only way to learn or get better was to DO. Most of my training is from the theater world. I participated in anywhere from one to six stage productions a year from elementary school through college. I also felt like it was important to learn all aspects of the craft, so my training included lighting, sound, costume, and set design. After I moved to LA and tried to transfer my stage skills to on-camera skills I took a similar approach. I took a few cold reading classes from a Casting Director who worked with the Disney Channel. I also did an extensive amount of background/extra and stand-in work on hundreds of TV shows and movies. I figured it was the best way to learn the differences between stage and on-camera acting, as well as pick up the differences in terminology and learn all the different jobs in film and TV. I looked at this as almost like a paid internship.

LL: Were your parents on board with your decision?

JE: I have the best parents in the world. While they couldn't help me financially to chase my dream, they always supported me and had faith that I would eventually reach my goals.

LL: Where did you grow up?

JE: I grew up outside Portland, Oregon in a town called Hillsboro. I went to Rocky Mountain College in Billings Montana. I think the six years I lived in Montana were the ones that gave me the confidence to move to LA and try to become an actor.

LL: Did you start your career there? Did your family move with you here to LA or did you come after you were 18?

JE: I would say I started my career in Montana. I had my first paid acting experiences there. I spent several summers in Virginia City, MT working for the Illustrious Virginia City Players. The biggest confidence builder came from working for The Montana Shakespeare In The Parks. It was an incredible group out of Montana State University-Bozeman and one my most memorable acting experiences. I didn't move to LA to act until after I had graduated with my degrees in both Theater and Biology and had spent those three summers doing paid theater.

LL: How did you get your first audition? Your first agent?

JE: I got my first agent by referral through Joey Paul Jensen. She was teaching the cold reading class I was taking. After about a month of classes she asked if I had an agent and good headshots. She called me in for an audition, helped me pick my headshots, then gave me a referral for an agent. The first audition was just a random audition for a guest star on a one hour drama. I didn't get it. LOL.

LL: What was your first paying acting job?

JE: My first paid acting gig was doing summer theater with The Illustrious Virginia City Players in Virginia City, Montana. My first paid acting gig in LA on-camera was on the show, *The Shield*. I had to shave my head and play a skin head who gets interrogated by Michael Chiklas.

LL: Were there any bumps along the way or surprises that you had to overcome?

JE: There are bumps everywhere and everything is a surprise! I have a youthful appearance which is good for acting in LA but my actual age kept being a problem. People would love me until they found out how old I really was. I began to understand that it's all about perception. It doesn't really matter how you see yourself, it's about what other people see in you. I could think I am the next **Tom Cruise** all I want, but if people see me as the next **Michael J. Fox** that's how you have to market yourself. I began to realize people will believe whatever age I told them and I could use that to reinforce the perception I wanted them to have (next Michael J. Fox). Once I began telling people I was eighteen, I started to work. I learned to match my most marketable skills (youthful, physical comedian, funny) with how people saw me and ended up booking Hannah Montana.

LL: How did you feel about auditioning?

JE: In general I hate auditioning, (laughs). I almost never feel like I have a great audition. I know that if I had the role, was on set, in wardrobe, acting with actors, taking direction, I would be perfect for the role. But, sometimes it gets discouraging in an office, when Casting Directors have already seen forty people, and they are clearly tired of being there. I used to take all the rejection personally. But then I realized there are a thousand factors on who gets cast from these auditions and very few of them have anything to do with me. I usually just audition now, then leave and forget I ever went. I try to look at it as a chance to practice. And if I do get the call that I booked the job...Bonus!!!!!

LL: Did you have one particular goal that you made early on in your career?

JE: I always wanted to be a series regular on a sitcom.

LL: Did you meet that goal?

JE: I met that goal not once, but twice. My proudest accomplishment is being a part of the best family show in the history of kid's television, *Hannah Montana*.

LL: Was there anyone who was particularly influential to you?

JE: I am a giant fan of Michael J. Fox. I watched everything he was in growing up and always thought we were similar types. He was a huge reason I wanted to be an actor.

LL: How did you get cast in *Hannah Montana*?

JE: *Hannah Montana* is the perfect example of how you just never know what to expect. When my agent called to tell me I had the audition, I read it and almost didn't go. I thought I was too old and didn't think there was any way I would even get a call back. It felt like a giant waste of time. My agents convinced me to go, saying that the industry is quiet at the moment, and there is nothing else going on, so just do it. Since I didn't think I had a shot, I just quickly went over the material but didn't over prepare.

When I got there, I remember you, Lisa, meeting me in the waiting area and told me that they were really looking for someone as close to the age of the character as possible (Jackson was sixteen) and to just tell them I was of legal age (meaning eighteen) if they asked. I did.

When I walked into the room to audition, I was surprised to see a bunch of Disney executives. One of them was very friendly and told me he remembered me from a previous show I did for Disney called *Phil of the Future*, and that he thought I was very funny. So there I am, auditioning for a show I didn't think I would get, in front of executives who already said they liked me, for a Casting Director who brought me in because I had auditioned well for her in the past and because of all that, I felt absolutely no pressure. It was one of my best auditions ever.

As I was leaving, you stopped me and asked if I would test for the network the next week. I did, and after just two auditions, I booked the role that changed my life. I learned that day that you never know when that life changing opportunity is going to come and what form it is going to take. You just have to go into everyday with an open mind and seize every chance as it comes. Every day is like playing the lottery and Hannah Montana was my one-in-a-million.

WORKSHEET:

When you've got your headshots and resume together, you're ready to create accounts and submit yourself on the actor online submission websites that are appropriate to your location. Do your research on each possible website before you sign up. Here is the list of the websites from this chapter as a starting point:

- Actors Access: **www.actorsaccess.com**—this gives you access to all states. You just pick your region and sign up.

- LA Casting: **www.lacasting.com**—for projects casting in Los Angeles.

- San Francisco: **www.sfcasting.com**—for projects casting in the San Francisco area.

- Casting Networks: **www.castingnetworks.com**—for other states outside of California or other countries.

- Now Casting: **www.nowcasting.com**—for projects all over the country, just pick your primary location

- Casting Frontier: **www.castingfrontier.com**—just pick the region you live in.

- Cazt: **www.cazt.com**

- The People's Network: **www.thepeoplesnetwork.com**

Chapter 6

THE ROLE OF AGENTS AND MANAGERS

Understanding the Talent Agent and Manager

A Talent Agency is an organization that represents various kinds of entertainment personnel in seeking employment and in business negotiations. Some talent agencies are franchised meaning they agree to the rules of the Screen Actors Guild (SAG)/AFTRA. This means they will negotiate for their clients' financial terms and working conditions that meet the basic requirements mandated by the guilds. For these services, franchised agencies receive ten percent of their client's gross pay. You can see whether an agency is franchised or not from the SAG website for your state.

There are also legitimate talent agencies that are not franchised by any of the guilds. While not subject to the minimum requirements set by SAG/AFTRA, they may be subject to regulations set by your state. For example, in California, non-franchised agencies can charge up to, but not more, than 20 percent of their client's gross pay.

A Talent Agent works for an agency (or has his/her own agency) and covers the functions listed below. A Talent Agent's job is to get you opportunities to go through the steps that will lead to acting jobs. Agents are in charge of selling talent, setting up auditions, getting your name and face out there to Casting Directors, Producers, and Directors, and handling the contracts once a job is secured. They will negotiate on your behalf, to make the deals. Selling is a main part of what Agents do; they are selling talent (the actor) and getting their talent seen. Basically they are there to open doors—to get you opportunities and then it's over to you, the Talent, to walk through those doors and get the job!

THEATRICAL AGENTS:

Agents submit actors for film, television (cable, network, and internet) and theater. They also do new media, web series, reality shows, etc. Some theatrical agents also submit their clients for commercials or have a commercial division within their agency.

COMMERCIAL AGENTS:

These are specialized agents who represent talent who do commercials, print, infomercials, hosting, reality shows, and new media, which includes "webisodes" and other internet web series. Some experienced hosts or comedians also do trade shows and game shows, and a commercial agent will represent them. If someone states that they are a commercial agency, essentially the only difference is that they don't submit you for film and television projects.

When you go in to see an Agent, be sure that you know whether they are a commercial or theatrical agent, or both. This will change how you discuss your career with them. To get a commercial agent, it is really about your personality and look. It's not that personality and look aren't part of theatrical auditions too, but there is more emphasis on what will be demanded of you as an actor. Keep in mind though, how creative some commercials are, and that many name actors become the spokesperson for different products, and this is why many actors have both a commercial and theatrical agent.

Sometimes, you can book a commercial that pays a lot of money in residuals. Residuals mean that every time the show or commercial airs on television, you get paid. This can give you the chance to continue your acting classes, get new headshots if you need them, etc. Don't look down on doing commercials because they are a great starting point.

There is no rule as to which Agent you should get first. For many young actors, acquiring a commercial agent is the way to get started. Even with no credits, it can be a little easier for a commercial agent to take a chance on you. Then you get the experience of going out for auditions, of which there can be many. It's a chance to get your feet wet, get used to going to auditions, meeting Casting Directors and Directors, and being on a set without so many of the demands of a theatrical shoot.

Many commercial agents also cover television and film projects. But the commercial agents who only cover commercials, move at a very fast pace because it is a very busy industry. You often get auditions for the same day or the next day and the commercial could even shoot that same week that you auditioned. Whether you are meeting a commercial or theatrical agent, you should always be prepared—show up on time, show that you are competent and committed.

It is also true that many good Directors started out directing commercials, so it's a great chance to start developing those relationships that may grow over the years to give you the film and television career you desire.

THE ROLE OF THE PERSONAL MANAGER

A Manager, per the dictionary, is a person who manages; has control of the activities, business dealings and other aspects of the career of an entertainer. They also help to develop talent. Often when you're first starting out, they will help with finding a good photographer for your head shots, getting you set up on different internet sites, and some may even assist with rehearsing for your auditions. Managers also help to attain your goals as an actor and will work much more closely with you in guiding your career. Managers might also help put promotional materials together to send to Casting Directors and teach you how to actually promote yourself. In the beginning of your career, this is really important.

They do have some different functions but as a person starting out, Agents and Managers do many of the same actions. Depending on the particular Agent or Manager, they are both important in helping guide you as an actor. Some Managers are more hands-on and like to recommend classes, photographers, etc. Some Agents will only take on people who are already further along in their careers. Both Agents and Managers are there to guide and get you opportunities. Many times an Agent or a Manager will take on a completely new actor because they really see potential—they see that you are focused and determined. That can work out really well because they have done this before and they like to nurture young talent. You have to discover for yourself if the Agent or Manager you are going to meet with is a good fit, depending on where you are at in your career. Both are exceedingly important for success in this business. They are part of your team.

An Agent usually has lots of people on his roster, it could be as many as fifty or sixty clients. Some larger agencies have hundreds of clients. Agents aren't always going to have the time to give you the personal attention you need—especially when starting out.

A Manager is someone who usually has a much smaller number of clients, can work more closely with you especially while building your career.

Most Agents are licensed with the Association of Talent Agents and as described earlier, charge 10%. Sometimes, an Agent will get 20% commission when you book a non-union job depending on what it is.

This is something that you can discuss with the Agent when meeting with them, and they will give you details on the commission rates.

Managers, on the other hand, are not licensed and can charge usually anywhere from 10% to 15%, and there are no requirements to be a Manager. I know a number of moms who helped their kids with their careers and were considered their kid's manager. They are now called "Momagers". Then they started managing other kids, teens and adults after that.

THE SIMILARITIES BETWEEN THE AGENT AND MANAGER:

In reality they are both there to help you get work. Agents and Managers both submit their clients, make phone calls to pitch their talent, and care deeply that you succeed. Managers are theoretically NOT allowed to negotiate. They do help the Agent and give advice regarding negotiations. However, if you have no Agent, a Manager will negotiate a deal for you.

Sometimes a Manager will help you get an Agent, they may already have good relationships with several around your town and will make a call to get you seen. Likewise, some Agents can assist you in getting a Manager if they think you need one. They are both looking out not only for your talent, but also your marketability. Remember, this is a business and everyone wants to make money.

Along this line, if an Agent or Manager has too many actors of a type that are similar to you, they will probably be less likely to take you on. It becomes a conflict of interest for them and they may have already invested months of work promoting the other actors. For example, if they were going to call a Casting Director and pitch a young attractive girl in her late teens, a type they may have two or more of, they would have to decide who to pitch. They would have to think about the girls who are very similar and probably would go with the one who books more jobs.

They are not going to pitch lots of people for the same role. It's about how much time the Manager or Agent can keep the Casting Director on the phone—these are very busy

[handwritten in left margin: a lot of Brunette Girls ::)]

people with much to do and a very short amount of time to do it.

People always ask me if they should get an Agent or a Manager. I always tell them, it's a personal choice. Some people get Agents first and likewise some choose a Manager first. There's no right or wrong answer here. It's all about your developing a personal relationship with both of these representatives.

Screen Actors Guild Information: SAG/AFTRA

The Screen Actors Guild is the union which represents professional actors and broadcasters. They merged with AFTRA (American Federation of Television and Radio Artists) in 2012. Headquartered in Los Angeles, SAG/AFTRA has 25 locales across the country to serve their members, signatory producers, and other industry professionals. As an actor, you become eligible for membership in SAG after you have gotten a union job. You don't have to join right away, because starting out there are many non-union jobs that you can audition for. Go to the SAG website and educate yourself on what the union does for its members and how to join when you are ready.

In addition to its main offices in Hollywood, SAG also maintains local branches in several major US cities, including Atlanta, Boston, Chicago, Dallas, Denver, Detroit, Honolulu, Houston, Las Vegas, Miami, Nashville, New York City, Philadelphia, Phoenix, Portland, Salt Lake City, San Diego, San Francisco, Seattle, and Washington, D.C.

On the Internet, search for Screen Actors Guild **www.sag.org** and then type in "Search Agents" (**http://www.sagaftra.org/agency-relations/sag-franchised-agents**). It will take you to a link that says "Find an Agent". Go to the bottom of the page, just below where it says "Search for an Agent". Use the drop-down menu to find and click on the state you live in. It may or may not have results you can then check out. Once you have clicked on your state, if there are no results, you might want to see if anything is available in the non-franchised **ATA/NATR** Association of Talent Agents and see what comes up. This will give you names, addresses, and phone numbers for Agents you can contact.

[**ATA**: Association of Talent Agents. **NATR**: National Association of Talent Representatives]

You need to be a bit of a detective and find out who is going to get you to your next step.

Here is an interview I did with an agent, **Pamela Fisher**, head of the Youth Division at Abrams Artists Agency. They are known for representing young talent and developing them into stars.

Lisa London: What is the difference between an agent and a manager?

Pamela Fisher: It's a very different world right now. There was a time, when a manager did more of the grooming; here's the photographer, here's the classes I think you should take… they would decide on the hairstyle, the look, etc. The agent was more of just getting the appointments. But now, there's so much more crossover. Agents become managers— managers become agents—and there was also a time when a casting director didn't give an appointment or a booking to a manager. Now those lines have blurred. So it's difficult to define the roles as to what an agent or manager is. But those two people should work well together in concert with your child's best interests. Sometimes when you have an agent, bringing on a manager is just another set of eyeballs, another team member because you feel you want to have that team support and hopefully they bring something different to the table than your agent. Some people have managers because they have musical aspirations, maybe they want to write, and the management company has a musical department or a literary division.

LL: What do you look for when you're meeting a potential new client?

PF: First of all, I'm looking for talent and an immediate reaction that we get from the actor. We're a much more in-the-gut business—something that is just a gut response to the talent and that's part of what we're trained to do. To identify it, feel that fire in the belly and the excitement that we see in the kid. There is the personality, no question. Sometimes we will sign a child that we've fallen in love with even though the audition might not have been spot on. I think that when they come in, myself and any Casting Director is forming an opinion the moment that actor walks through the door. What they do in the room can be even more important than the audition. And I've had that happen, where you just fall in love with a kid and you just feel there is something there.

Obviously, a six year old doesn't come in with a body of work—the adult division gets to watch a reel and see what the actor has done with their careers. But we're also looking for something that is missing on our list of clients, even if I respond favorably to a child, and they are amazing. But if they are an eleven year old blond girl with blue eyes and I have six of that type on my list that aren't working, it just wouldn't be fair to take on someone else in this category. If it's someone I need, then it's exciting to me, because obviously that child is going to have a lot of exclusivity.

LL: What should an actor have prepared when they come to see you?

PF: I like to see a monologue or a scene. I think that a lot of agents in town use cold readings. I'm not a huge fan of the cold read because I feel that the child is so rarely asked to do it. Generally, if you have an agent or a manager and you're sent on an audition, you have a chance to review the material ahead of time. I prefer to see what's going to happen when the child has the time to review the material, rather than see how talented they are at cold reads, I love to see what they can do. I don't think that I am the norm though. I do think that many people who go into agencies and management offices will find that their child is handed a cold read. They might want to work on that skill as well.

You can find lots of monologues online or you can look up your child's favorite show and look up a scene or script from it and we always have someone who can read with them. They don't need to bring somebody to read the scene with them—we always have someone or I can read with them. But I would prefer to see what they do with something they have had time to work on.

LL: If they sing, or have a little stand-up routine—would you have them do that?

PF: Yes, absolutely, I would have them do that. This is their time—show me what you've got. I want to know everything I can in as short a period of time as I can. I think even in a cold read situation there is nothing wrong with having your child prepared with a scene or monologue. It's always a good thing to have in your back pocket, to whip out.

LL: At what point, when meeting a young actor, do you meet the parents?

PF: I do come out and meet the parents, and if I'm super interested in the child, I might bring the parents in to chat. It's very important, because we're representing not just kids, but families. This is hopefully going to be a long-term relationship. It's something where we're going to groom your child and I definitely want to get to know the parents and who we're getting involved with. So first, I'm looking to see is the child open to separating from their parents in their audition? Is there any anxiety involved with that? One of the things I generally ask very quickly to the young actor when we are alone, "So, you want to be an actor? What made you want to be in this Industry?" We do have countless unfortunate situations where the child answers that they don't want to. Their Mom or Dad really want them to be actors, or are pushing them. At which point, we see their audition and we tell them what a great job they did and we say thank you. We always want to make sure that it's absolutely something the kid wants.

LL: What feedback do you give to parents?

PF: In this situation, if the parent really pushes me I would probably say, it's not the right match right now. I don't want to discourage the family. But other times if I'm really pressured for specifics, I may say what was said in the room, that it's not really something he/she wants to do, so you might want to reevaluate that with your child.

Sometimes we meet with a young actor and there is some really good feedback that can be given, and when there is I will e-mail it. The other day I had a ten year old girl that played with her sweater the entire audition. I wrote to the Mom and said she has great potential. "I would like her to go and work with somebody specifically on focus. She didn't know where to look in the room. And don't have her wear that sweater. She played with the sleeves on the sweater the entire time." When I can give something like that, it's a wonderful teachable moment and it's great. I'm happy to impart that information and to help. Because there is something there and they should continue, and I want to encourage that.

LL: Are there any questions you usually ask the potential client?

PF: I want to warm them up so I try to take their minds off the fact that they are in this uncomfortable situation with a stranger. We tell our children all their lives "Don't talk to strangers." Then you separate them and send them into a room in a big agency with strangers. We try to calm them down, and ask them questions about their lives. They should be prepared to answer with more than a "yes" or "no". So if I say "You go to school at... is it fun?" And the young actor says yes or no, that's it—it closes the door, there's nothing to be said. Whereas the child should be prepared with answers that show who they are.

At the end of the day there's going to be hundreds of kids we meet that can read the lines with expression. It's what this child brings to the meeting that is a little bit different, a little bit special, a little bit unique. That makes them stand apart. If there's something interesting that they can say. If I ask, "Hey, you drove all the way in from... did you have a good trip?" They can say "yes, and along the way, we did such and such... I sang a song in the car and I was rehearsing, and I was so excited..." just something to open the conversation.

The more you can work with your child and mock up auditions, the more comfortable they will be. At home, have them enter a room and sit down, then ask them all sorts of questions. I always ask them what their favorite shows are, what they like to watch on television. I want to know if they are watching the shows my clients are on. It gives us tremendous insight. Kids say crazy things sometimes. But it makes the potential client memorable. I want it to be an honest response, but I think they should be open to have good, fun, open banter.

LL: What questions should the actor or the parents ask the agent when deciding if they should sign with them?

PF: I think it's totally appropriate to ask if there are a lot of conflicts for you as the young actor or your child. How many clients are on the roster, are there a ton of people who are similar to you, do you think there will be some exclusivity? I mean, we have to be realistic about it, obviously, you or your child will be one of a few. You want to make sure this is a situation where there is going to be the attention needed.

LL: If I'm a teenager—say I'm 15 and I come in to see you—are there any other questions that I should be thinking of to ask you?

PF: To get started—so if we're going to work together, we're going to make sure—do you like the picture? What do you think of my headshot? What is your policy of phone calls and visiting? Because I want to manage the expectations here—some people feel very disconnected. The agent is very, very busy. We have an unusual situation here, at my agency, in that we have an open door policy. Specifically because of that, in a world of many agencies, we wanted to see what we could do that would set us apart. A lot of people felt very disconnected. I can't get in touch with my agent… I can't get them on the phone… I can't even come to see them, etc. Because we're very busy, it's an endless job.

It's hard if we're spending time on the phone constantly with the parents and the teenagers, and they are constantly in the office, when are we getting the work done? Wouldn't you prefer that I was pitching you? But in the same vein, we do offer an open door policy. We do respond to e-mails immediately and we get on the phone with the client and the parents, but it does make for a longer day. But we like them to feel connected and I think that has to be taken within reason, so you have to make sure you're not badgering the agent.

But if you or your parent are very needy and you're going to want that kind of relationship, you'll have to think, what are the things I need before I go into an agency? Because as much as we're looking at you to see what we need, this is your business. You are your business! I need someone who is just getting me the work. Or, I need someone who I can get on the phone. Or I need someone who's going to be a partner with me in this. For parents and kids, it's really good to be clear on what it is that you want out of the relationship. Because I do think that an agent should be honest with you.

Another agent might say you cannot come by here anytime you want. No, we are not going to be on the phone with you every day. We're not there to hold your hand in that respect. It's good to know ahead of time what's going to work for you. Because to just sign on with an agency that's not going to be right, you don't want to get known as the person who is hopping around from agent to manager to agent. Hopefully, it's a long-term relationship.

LL: Do they ever ask you, "how often can I expect to go on auditions?"

PF: I get asked constantly, "how many times a week should I expect to go out?" I have no crystal ball to know. You may go out so much—we have some people who cannot go to all their auditions. We have to cancel because it's so crazy that week. And then you may not hear from us for two weeks. I wish I could look into the crystal ball and see, but I don't know what projects they are writing right now that are going to have 11 year old Hispanic boy in them in the next few weeks. It could be nothing and there could be a million things.

LL: At what point do you think that an actor is ready to take on an agent? If you meet them and you feel they aren't ready, what do you do? What advice do you give?

PF: We always give really specific feedback. And if we're interested, we think there is something there, but they're not quite ready yet. The most unfortunate situation we could have is that we take somebody on and send your child out, even if there's a ton of raw talent there, but we know it's not going to work in the room. They just don't know where to look or what to say, or how to behave in the room. We'll tell the parent. There's not a ton of work to be done here—we're close—but it's not quite ready. If we send them in, the worst situation is that the Casting Director makes a note that they are not ready and then it is hard to get them back in that room again. "Oh, I've already read such 'n such and they are too green." We want to make sure that when you walk in—you're ready. Not only because we want to make a fan of the Casting Director, but also because of how the child feels about themselves is so important. Even a kid knows when they are not prepared and when they are not ready.

A kid who walks in confidently and knows what to do is ideal. I know where to look, and I know how to behave in the room. There's a different kind of confidence that goes in and allows the Casting Director or the Producer to relax. Whereas going in before being ready, and I know the parent is so excited to have a talented child and wants to push them… "They're ready, send them in… everyone will love them." But truly, I can't stress it enough that sometimes it's better to take a little bit more time to make sure that child is prepared. I'm happy to recommend a class, or a coach for them to work with. And I'll say go ahead for the next 6 months and study, let's reevaluate. I'll leave the door open. It's just that I'm not ready to sign them now. We've had situations where other agencies are ready, and the actor will go with somebody else. We feel sad that we've lost the talent, but I really wouldn't feel confident sending them out yet, because our reputation is on the line too. I don't want the Casting Director to say, "What were you thinking?"

LL: What do you suggest to people who want to move to LA?

PF: That is always difficult because then it's sitting on my shoulders that a family is going to relocate. We're going to work very hard, to try to get them out here. We had people coming from out of town and I remember one year, there was not one pilot with a kid in it. I would say to make the best of your experience if you're going to come out. Don't think so much about booking the job, but think of it as an educational experience. If that's okay for you, then make the move but know that you are going to use that time to take classes, Casting Director workshops and get some coaching.

Those first auditions that you get, are of part of the learning curve. I know a lot of parents get hung up on, "Oh, I heard if you go out on five auditions and you only get three call backs that the ratio will be off and you'll drop us." It doesn't quite work that way. We know that those first auditions are very fish out of water, and new. Use these as a learning experience, manage the expectations appropriately so that you know, it's probably not that you're going to come out and land a show on your first audition. Having said that, it's always very exciting—it does happen—a kid came out from Alabama, he put himself on tape actually in Alabama, and they flew him out, and he auditioned and he booked a series.

LL: Do people ever send you auditions from Alabama or some other state, and ask for you to represent them?

PF: Sometimes, they'll make themselves a little reel of themselves doing some material…

LL: So you would look at it and you would tell them when they come out to LA we'd love to meet with you?

PF: Yes, absolutely, absolutely.

LL: Is there anything you do to help actors get more auditions or call backs and bookings?

PF: Sometimes, it's the picture that is not working. If it's a picture that I chose that I really like, maybe I made a mistake and for whatever reason casting isn't responding as much as I had thought or hoped—let's choose a different one and put it up there and see what happens. Sometimes that can help because Casting Directors are looking at these thumbnail pictures that come up in the submissions. In addition they are getting e-mails, calls from the agents and managers. Getting a picture that is right and that gets the right response can help.

Also, we try to get the feedback to know what went wrong in the room. And we love getting feedback. Even something that might seem negative to the parent or the actor, that's wonderful, that's gold. It's wonderful to hear it was something they were wearing or someplace that they were looking, or whatever it is that's specific, because that is fixable.

Sometimes, it's very tough, because often there's just not a reason. Parents really want that reason, and sometimes there isn't one. You didn't get it because somebody else did. "You know we had other choices," is a big answer that Casting Directors give. I think that's very truthful, they had a different choice. It's not because of anything that your child did. When we do get the feedback, we can help by getting them to a coach and work on that specific issue and problem.

But it is an art and that is how it is. It's difficult sometimes for parents and for people who work in other industries where the answers are very clear. Art is so subjective that sometimes there isn't really a specific answer. I believe the Casting Director when they say, "Different choice, different way." Don't get hung up on that project, know that the feedback was good. The Casting Director said it was a good job. You made a fan. Go in—make a fan—they will remember you. That's the Casting Director's job is to have that type of memory so that they're able to, in the next thing they're casting, to think of you and call you in. This is development. It's not about booking immediately always. It's about making fans. If you're coming here from out-of-town, if you're new to the industry—get out—get in rooms—start to make fans.

LL: Do you recommend Casting Director workshops?

PF: I like Casting Director workshops. I know that they can be pricey and you're probably not going to get a very deep acting theory lesson, but you will get a quick response to what you are doing in the room, how you're doing in the audition space. The Casting Director might give you a note on your picture or sometimes they will give you something that is concrete to work on about your audition. And if you do a good job, they will put you in their files. And I don't mind if it's the associate or the assistant. We have had people get in to more auditions that way. They'll get called in from those workshops.

LL: Do you recommend acting classes, improv, singing or dancing classes to actors starting out?

PF: Definitely! I recommend being as well-rounded as you can be. Being up in front of each other, watching each other; learn from the people you are friends with who are also in your class, watch what they're doing. Class doesn't end when your scene is over. Definitely, go do other things as well. I had somebody come in the other day and she was fifteen and said, "My whole life, this is all I've ever done. I've taken every acting class, I've gone to New York, I've taken every possible drama class. I've never done anything else but acting—it's my whole life. I read books on acting all day." And I wanted to say to her—go learn to horseback ride—go to Europe… I think there's nothing to bring to the acting… you've done all this. You need to be a well-rounded person. It's difficult to draw from life's experiences if there really isn't anything else you're doing. I'm OK if you love karate, or you love baseball. And I'm OK if you're a chef, so go and enjoy your life experiences.

LL: What advice would you give to young actors who are just starting their journey?

PF: I think it's smart to remember that this is a business. It's a good dream, but you also have to know that there is a business side to it, so there has to be a balance in your life between the excitement and the dream and the reality. One of the hardest things to do, is to continuously feel good about yourself. If you know you're good, don't let anyone else tell you what you are, what you're not. Go for it, but listen to the feedback. Work hard, and just keep the goal in front of you and don't let anything distract you or get you down.

I do think that some actors, when they feel defeated, bring that into the room with them. There's sometimes an oppressive air in the audition space. You can tell the actor is going in feeling defeated, not feeling good about themselves. Go in prepared, feel great. Psych yourself up to go in and do a great job. And leave great work in the room and walk away and forget about it. I think obsessing about it is always the worst part. What happened?—Why didn't they call me—"I gotta know…" Go in do a great job then move on! Let it be something else that you did in your day and move on.

LL: And if it's your passion, your dream, don't stop believing!

PF: Yep, keep going. We have people who stay with us for years—it's just not happening, but we know that there is something there. It may not be this year, or next year, or the year after that. But the year after that they're booking a show. We just know it—they're booking a movie. So keep at it. Sometimes things cycle around. It's not the right age, it's not the right time…

LL: Any tidbits or stories about how you helped a child get started and they became a series regular, or in a big movie?

PF: I think the joy of developing in general is so wonderful. You want to find a manager or agent who actually enjoys what they are doing. When I was a junior (agent) working under Bonnie Liedtke, one of the first times that I felt and saw what this industry can do and watched something happen was with **Zac Efron**. He was a round, chubby-faced kid with a big split between his teeth and he was an excellent actor. He played some roles where he was mentally challenged. Watching that change through the television series, "Summerland", going into "High School Musical" and seeing pretty much overnight, what that did in this child's life and to his family was great. From one day to the next, he would come up to the office to visit us and there would be paparazzi downstairs and deliveries of clothing from designers. Would he wear this?

What happened "overnight" and seeing that change, and seeing the power of this business, was a very exciting time for someone coming up through the ranks as an agent. Being able to do that for other people's careers was exciting to me. Developing **Ariana Grande** and watching what she did when we first put her on *Victorious*, the excitement and joy. Again, someone changing "overnight"—watching someone's life go from not being known and anonymity to suddenly she's got 6.5 million Twitter followers. We started out with her—she was thirteen or fourteen, having just done a Broadway show that a friend of mine was the composer on. And we got the introduction to her, met her and fell in love with her. Watching her change from her curly brown hair and then all of a sudden she was this pink-haired girl on a television series. I fall in love with my clients. I'm doing this again with a girl named **Dove Cameron** who is starring in a new show for the Disney Channel, *Liv and Maddie*, and she's going to play twins against herself, which hasn't been done since *Parent Trap*.

LL: And she was someone you developed?

PF: Completely. It's taken a couple of years but it was someone that I really felt that feeling about. You just know it in the room and I said to her Mom, "She's going to be huge. There's something very, very special—you just know." And I knew when I met this girl.

LL: You knew she would be special…. Sometimes we talk about the "It" factor.

PF: And you have a responsibility to it. She was fourteen to fifteen years old. You have a responsibility to a parent and the child to not raise their hopes. But I needed to tell this Mom and Dove that this was going to happen. I just knew and we had to prepare. It was an instinct.

LL: Any final thoughts?

PF: This is a very unusual relationship, it's a relationship that is both personal and professional and you don't see a lot of that. You need to know that you trust the person who is your manager or agent. Do I feel that I trust this person? At the end of the day, unless it's some agency that no one has ever heard of, or if it's an agency that asks for money up front—Don't Ever. That's obviously a big red flag. From some little agency right up to the top, we all use the same breakdowns, we all get the same information. Some agencies like to say we have a better relationship with studios, or I know the projects better. But we really all get the information the same. This is a big information age. It's really who do you connect with—who do you want in there fighting for you? And if it's some little boutique agency, but that person is passionate about your child and you just connect with that person, better to go with them. Even though the biggest agency is interested in your child, and you didn't feel close to them, it's more important to go where the passion is, where you feel comfortable. Trust your instinct as a parent—you've probably done a pretty good job. I'd say trust your instincts and go with your heart when you're choosing an agent or manager.

Worksheet:

ONLINE RESEARCH FOR AGENTS AND MANAGERS:

Take the time to do your homework. Use the internet to research Agents and Managers.

If you're looking for an Agent outside of New York or Los Angeles, you can search for a list of Agents by city using the Screen Actors Guild website:

http://www.sagaftra.org/agency-relations/sag-franchised-agents

If you live in small town, you would type in the name of the largest city nearest you and type in "talent agents" and see what comes up. Sometimes, these agencies will not be SAG-franchised agents. They can still be legitimate agencies and can be a good start for you.

Enter "Actors Managers" in the search window or "Directory of Talent Agents" to see what's currently available.

You can view contact data and information of Talent Managers that belong to the Talent Managers Association on their website:

http://www.talentmanagers.org/

You can view the contact data for members of the Association of Talent Agents on their website:

http://www.agentassociation.com/frontdoor/membership_directory.cfm

Take the time to get an agency or manager guide. As a young talent, I would look though the agency book and highlight the agents who represent children, (CH= children, COM= commercial, PRT= print, TH= Theatrical).

The Samuel French Bookstore is an excellent resource to purchase theatrical and film scripts as well as books on acting including directories of agents and managers: **http://www.samuelfrench.com**

7

GETTING AN AGENT OR MANAGER

Now you have done some research and decided who you want to send your picture and resumes to. These are suggestions on how to go about this:

Find a name of someone at the talent agency, then send your picture and resume to that particular agent. Don't just send it to three to five people at the same agency. Pick a name and if you are under eighteen be sure they represent young talent. Send them out to many agencies—don't be afraid to send those headshots out—that's why you got them made! Send it with a short personal note, I always tell actors to mail or e-mail your picture and resume to a specific person.

Your note could say that you are passionate about acting or just did a play, or invite them to a showcase. Let them know you are available and would love to meet with them. Not your life history, just a short note. For example:

"I've heard great things about your agency, would love to meet you because I feel I could be an asset to you."

Another way to research Agents and Managers is to talk to your acting teacher, or other actors in the class and find out who represents them or if they can get you a meeting with the Agent. Ask your teacher if she knows any Agents or Managers that perhaps she would set you up with. There are so many successful stories of how networking in this way can really start the ball rolling. This is about asking for help and persisting in doing the work, and the rest will pay off.

Take the example of a sixteen year old girl whom I cast in her first pilot and movie. She was acting in a Community Theater show and the Director had a friend who was a Manager and invited her to see the play. The Manager loved her and took her on as a client. When the part in the pilot came up, the Manager called me and pitched her. We met with her and the rest is history.

Getting an Agent or Manager is not only about your talent, but also about your passion. It plays a huge role in acquiring representation. Make it something you eat, sleep, and breathe daily! Your passion, personality, and persistence will help you to succeed as an actor. There may always be someone taller, prettier, more handsome and maybe even more talented. But you can be quirky, funny, offbeat, diverse, unique, or even an amazing singer. It is your excitement, dedication, and talent that will convince the Agent or Manager to take you on as a client! Believe in yourself and convince others to believe in you—inspire them to take a chance on representing you.

DECIDING ON AN AGENT OR MANAGER

Who really "gets" you? Who will really help you to reach your goals? You have to go on instinct and when you get a meeting, evaluate whether you can work with this Agent and if they believe in you.

I wouldn't go with an Agent that I felt I couldn't talk openly with regarding my goals or my challenges. They may disagree with the way to get to those goals. They may also see you differently than you see yourself, and this can work in your favor. Sometimes through the help of an Agent or Manager, an actor will realize they can play roles that they didn't think were right for them. So be open to their feedback.

To play the devil's advocate: how **DO** they see your upcoming future. You may think you're a leading man and they only see you as a character type. Be sure to discuss this in your interviews so you are both on the same page. You may think you would be perfect for mainstream TV and they think you should audition for quirky independent cable and film projects.

They may also have to tell you at some point that you didn't get the part and have criticisms or directions that came from the Casting Director or Director. Take these directions and don't argue with your representation. They are on your side. You become a team with them and they should be rooting for you. It's not a successful relationship if you don't trust the Agent or Manager's judgment or have a sense that they are not on your side. You want to be in sync with your Agent or Manager because they are guiding your career and you both need to be moving in the same direction. Also, there is a lot of leg work in the beginning—bringing your headshots to them, creating your resume, (they might have changes on the resume about how to make you look your best) marketing, getting you in to see an important Casting Director, etc.

When you're just starting out you might be so happy to have gotten a meeting with the one agent located in your town that you'll do everything you can to make it a good fit. But even if this is the only agent in town, ask how they feel about getting calls to see what's going on around town—audition-wise. Once you have secured an Agent and find that you haven't gotten any auditions, you might want to call and remind them that you are still out there and want to work. You don't have to bug them and call all the time, but you do want to stay in good communication with them. Dropping by periodically to say "Hi" to your Agent or Manager or having a meeting with them every once in a while is a good thing so that you stay fresh in their minds. Also, bringing muffins or some treat doesn't hurt, even to the assistants who do a lot of legwork on your behalf.

YOU HAVE GOTTEN A MEETING WITH AN AGENT OR MANAGER.

Here's what happens next:

During the interview you may be asked to do a monologue or a cold reading. You may also be asked to come back and meet other Agents at the agency or it might all take place in one meeting. The interview can go either way, so be prepared for all of it.

PREPARING FOR THE MEETING:

Bring your picture and resume.

Prepare two, one minute monologues—one comedic and one dramatic. You might not be asked to do these, but it is good to have them in your back pocket. You can also tell the Agent or Manager in the meeting that you have prepared a monologue for them and ask them if they would they like to see it.

If you sing, have a song prepared. You might only be asked to sing a few verses, but be prepared with the whole song.

Bring any tape, CD, or DVD that could show your previous work. If you had a good role in a play that was recorded in good quality where it shows your acting (not from a mile away), then get a copy and have it edited with your strongest scenes.

If you have done a piece that is on YouTube that you are proud of, now would be the time to show it to the Agent or Manager you are meeting with.

You could also have a scene you have rehearsed with another person, and bring that for them to see. Before you go to the meeting, ensure that the Agent or Manager knows that you have a scene with another person and you're ready to do it for them. Don't just spring this on them at the **meeting!** Sometimes Agents are only going to give you a short amount of time, so make sure your plan is discussed ahead of time.

Be prepared to do a cold reading. Both theatrical and commercial Agents and Managers might have you do cold readings. This is when they give you copy (material from a commercial or TV show) that you have never seen before and give you a couple of minutes to go over it. Bring your reading skills and creativity with you!

When you do a scene for an Agent in their office, here are some dos and don'ts:

Pick a scene that is simple and shows your "castability". Something that you could actually be cast in and again... age appropriate.

- Keep it under five minutes

- Don't use props, special effects, guns, knives, etc.

- Do not be too sexy

- No kissing or making out

You want to dazzle the Agents or Managers, not intimidate them. Don't forget that the space is different in an office than in the theater. This is where you show your personality, charm and talent. You want them to represent you and be excited about having you on their client list. Go in there with a positive attitude and a winning smile. Don't forget, this is the entertainment industry and everyone likes to be entertained.

If an Agent or Manager agrees to meet with you, there is something about your picture, resume or pitch that has intrigued him or her enough to do so. It could also be that a Casting

Director, Producer, or Director recommended that he meet with you. If he or she tells you that they won't be able to represent you, it is okay to ask perhaps, "how come?" You cannot get upset, because people move around a lot in this industry. One day he is an Agent with fifty or more clients and the next day he is a Manager looking for talent. If you are rude or get very upset if they don't take you on, then that leaves a bad impression. If you leave graciously, then down the road, that Agent may just call you in again if his circumstances change. He may have had too many people in your category or just didn't feel you had enough experience at that time. But six months later, many things can change and you have to always keep a positive outlook.

QUESTIONS FOR THE MEETING WITH AN AGENT OR MANAGER:

You might ask them:

1. Have they taken someone from where I am to the next level, and how do they see this going?

2. Do they have good relationships with many of the Casting Directors in town?

3. Do they think I am viable?

4. What kind of roles do they see me playing?

5. Will they pick up the phone and make calls to pitch me?

6. Will they pick up the phone and talk to me when I call?

Some Agents don't like it if you call and bug them about getting auditions, so this is good to know up front. It's bad etiquette to call your Agent or Manager every day—unless they have told you to do so. They are usually too busy trying to get you seen!

7. Can I drop by unannounced?

8. How many clients does that Agent or Manager handle?

It is a good idea to do your research before you meet with the Agent or Manager.

How many clients do they have that are similar to me? You should research what kind of clients that Agent has on your own before you meet with them. Go to the SAG website or imdb.com (Internet Movie Database) and look at what clients they have. Managers can be accessed through their own websites or you can look them up on imdb.com.

These are the kinds of questions you want to ask yourself after the meeting:

1. How interested did he/she seem upon meeting me?

2. Did he ask me some personal questions about myself and my goals?

3. Did he/she ask me about classes I'm taking or have taken?

4. Did I feel I communicated my passion for performing?

5. Did I really show them my personality?

6. Did his or her viewpoint enlighten me in some way?

7. Did I feel confident that he or she would represent me and that we could be a team?

8. Was I excited about my future with this Agent or Manager?

These are just a sample of some questions; it is up to you to formulate your own based on what you would like to know.

Remember, this is your interview, so it is up to you how you want it to go. If your interview at first seems boring or un-dynamic, then it is up to you to change it and become more interested and animated. This is one of the first steps to your career and it is an important interview. You need to go in with a good attitude, be excited sincerely (not phony). Be interested in the person you are interviewing with. If at first it seems a little awkward, find something that you can admire or are interested in about the person. For example, you admire some of his or her clients, you see a picture on the wall of a movie poster that you really like, and ask about it. Did he have a client in it or is it just a favorite movie of his/her's?

Sometimes, being interested in the person in front of you, makes you even more appealing. An interview is a two-way street. Remember, just be yourself!!

Interview with Bonnie Liedtke:

Bonnie Liedtke's track record of breaking young talent comes from her many years of experience as a top agent, and she is now a manager with Principato-Young Management. She handled the careers of young actors who went on to become major stars including, **Leonardo DiCaprio, Hilary Swank** and **Zac Efron**. She is presently the manager of **Sophia Grace** and **Rosie**, the young girl sensations from *The Ellen Show*. She shares some of her expertise here with us.

Lisa London: What is the difference, in your opinion, between an agent and a manager?

Bonnie Liedtke: I think that a manager is a little more fine detailed day-to-day. You are dealing with career and personal things, which they wouldn't necessarily tell the agent. You have a little bit more time to put into their careers and know the actor's personal preferences because you have less clients. As a manager I now know more about things I didn't know about as an agent.

LL: Do you think there is more crossover now between Managers and Agents, in the aspect of pitching or submitting?

BL: Yes, a lot of crossover. We pretty much do the same thing, it's just with less clients and a little bit more fine-tuned. For instance, I have a client now who has optioned three different projects, a short story, and two books. As an agent, it wasn't something that I probably would be that invested in. I would sometimes read them or send them to a department that would do that. But as a manager, now I have a much bigger opinion about it, where I'm looking at the big picture.

LL: What do you look for when you're meeting with a new potential client?

BL: Poise is always one of my favorite things. I do think that charm and poise is part of the package. And one part of that package is invisible, which is luck. I just can't explain what that magical ingredient is, but I do think there are so many things that factor in. Sometimes it can be a feeling inside my gut. Obviously, sometimes a look can be a magical look that works too. It might even be that a certain ethnicity walks in the room, and I need that. There are so many different elements that come into play.

LL: What should an actor have prepared for you when they come in to see you? Do they do scenes for you?

BL: They could have a couple of monologues. They could have put up a scene and taped it, from temple, church, school or an acting class. I'll look at a play. I would see a scene if they brought it in. I could go and see something. There are so many options.

LL: Normally would you have them tape something for you to see?

BL: These days when they send in a tape, and say, they live in England, I'll say—"You have a hundred times to get this tape right." Whereas if I send you into a Casting Director's office, you have one time—maybe a Casting Director will give you a second shot, but that is all you have. If you can't be 100% when you send me that tape, chances are that we're not going to work together, unless I can give you some advice and you re-tape and it's great. Nothing is more annoying than receiving a tape and the actor is looking at the pages. You have to be off book if you send in a tape. You have no choice—it's not an option. So you really have to put the goods all together and make it 100% when you're self-taping and sending it in. That goes for a Casting Director, Agent, or Manager. You have no excuse.

LL: Say you like somebody, and get that feeling for them. Do you have to get the OK from the other people in the office?

BL: If they are on tape, I would show it in the "Big Room" (the meeting room where all the managers get together), which is what we call it. They can see whoever it is that I am showcasing, and then I will give a little pitch. They don't necessarily all have to meet the actor. You're selling it to your colleagues and you're letting them know, this is why I like Suzy, because I saw her perform this, or I believe in her and this is what I love about her. Collectively we can talk about representing her, but usually they let me make a choice. An agency is completely different. They all have to agree, or maybe not all, but it's a much different situation.

LL: What kind of feedback do you give the parents? Do you bring them in?

BL: I give honest feedback and I do bring the parents in. That could take up to six months. It's a journey, and it's constantly changing. We find out different things about each other that they might not like about me, or I might not like about them. It becomes about telling them how things should be done differently. If it's "You brought four people to an audition—you can't do that." Or you said something inappropriate that really offset the room, or the Casting Director overheard you say something inappropriate. So yes, I will absolutely be honest. I'm not trying to be hurtful, I'm just trying to deliver the truth and make sure we don't do it again, so we correct it.

LL: Say you're meeting a client you are interested in—would you bring the parents in right away?

BL: Yes. That's important. I've had a lot of bad parents in the past.

LL: Can you define "bad parents".

BL: Bad Parents could push the child when he/she doesn't want to be pushed. It could be as easy as over committing the child—soccer, cheerleading, football, and acting. You can't do all of them. Maybe, it's that they are not taking my advice and putting the child into classes. They don't think the child needs a class. It could be so many different things— inappropriate dressing for the kid's age. Or they could bleach the child's hair—I've seen that done before, you can imagine there are hundreds of things. It could be being too bossy, thinking you know it all.

If they come in to me and they aren't realistic in how they see their child (as an ingénue, character, leading man, etc.), that's an immediate problem. If they are way off, it's probably the biggest point of how it's not going to be a great relationship. I will be honest with them and if we can't see eye to eye, it's just not meant to be. You have to be on the same page.

LL: Any specific questions you ask your potential clients?

BL: I like to hear they are reading things. When they are fifteen or sixteen, they need to start being aware of books that are going to be made into movies. Look at "Hunger Games". You need to bring things into the room so you can carry on a conversation to be interesting. You have to be well read—I think that's important. And to know about things that are going on around you. If you can't go into the room with people who have fought for this material, and know about it, you look like you just don't care.

I also like to know what films have inspired you. What films have you seen? I like to know what their personal interests are. Do they have certain hobbies that inspire them? I always ask if there is a charity that you work with—something that you like to do? Animal rescue, etc? What do you do? That's important.

I like people to be in acting class. I'm not saying they have to be; some people have the gift naturally and it doesn't need to be fine-tuned. Others just want to do privates, or be in *The Groundlings* (Improvisation Group and classes). Then as we go along and if we're getting certain feedback, I'll say "Your audition technique isn't good." You're not walking into the room and owning it. I always tell people, you've got 30 seconds to own it in the room, and make everybody in the room love you, and not everybody has the ability to do that. They like what you do in the room, but you're not making them feel comfortable, then we know we have to work on audition technique. Or if it's cold reading or improv—whatever it is, we try to fine-tune it as we go along. That's not easy, by the way, to find the right coach for every kid, or person. Everybody is different. I say to them, sit in on two or three different classes and then you choose. Sometimes they need a new technique and need to switch it up. I would say that 90% are in some kind of classes.

Know your heritage, know who you are. What nationality are you? A lot of young actors don't—it's one of my pet peeves. They could be extremely ethnic but they'll say I'm white. Somewhere along their bloodlines you came from somewhere else. And we need to try to figure out where that was, because it will help you with your career. I use **Taylor Lautner,** when he was doing *Twilight* as an example of this. We found out that he had Native American in his bloodline, and that was really important to him getting *Twilight*. If you do have something, (being ethnic) you are hurting yourself if you don't know it—you are cutting your career in half. We're looking for all ethnicities—it has become such a priority to us with the studios.

LL: What question should the young performer ask the Manager?

BL: The number one question they always ask is, do you have conflicts? Give me certain examples of careers you have started. Give me a couple of journeys. Young actors come in having done their research. There is so much access nowadays, they can Google everything. I think the really smart ones do read up. You have to be savvy.

LL: Is there a "don't" that you would tell young actors coming in to meeting with a Manager?

BL: I'm not big on props… I like when people look like they are supposed to look. So many people get their hair done, hair extensions, extra make-up—I don't want that. I've heard of Casting Directors who have washed actor's faces to try and get rid of the make-up. There is a good quote from an acting coach that I like and refer to: Show up dressed for the party. They want you to get the part. They've invited you to the party, now show up dressed and ready.

I've always thought that was true, because I'll have an actor whine to me about "the Casting Director doesn't like me… she was mean to me, she took a call when I was in the room…" But I said, she's bringing you back in for the second call. I tell them, she invited you back—I didn't push her to see you. Dress the part, show up. They stop themselves and get in their own way.

Don't come in wearing lots of perfume—or come in sick. This may seem like common sense but new actors should know this and reschedule if they are sick.

LL: At what point do you feel an actor is ready for a manager? And if you meet them and don't feel they are ready, do you tell them?

BL: 97% of the people I meet are ready for one or both. They've been recommended, they have been in classes. It's a little bit different, if I were just starting out, but I've been around doing this for over twenty-five years.. I have never been that dream crusher, I've never said to anybody, give up and change careers. Who knows, in two years they could come out of their shell and be ready.

LL: Have you ever had it where someone comes in to meet you and they are just not ready? What advice would you give them?

BL: If they are somewhat ready, and I can't sign them, then I send them to showcases. I think the local showcases are awesome. To be able to read in front of agents, managers and casting directors that you normally wouldn't have the opportunity if you didn't have representation is the best place you can do it. I've seen lots of people get great jobs from those things.

I think if they are really raw, I send them to classes. If it's more that they are just awkward and uncomfortable but their instincts are good, it's more audition technique classes. Sometimes it could be that they are not ready because they need a lot of teeth work, like getting braces. They may be really beautiful and should be leading ladies, not really characters, so they need to slim down. I've had to tell people on series that they have to slim down, or tell famous people they have to do something different. This is my job. The journey is my adventure with you to help you, and you have to listen to these things, because it will make a difference.

LL: Do you suggest to parents to move out here to LA?

BL: Very rarely. Especially now with the beauty of uploading auditions onto the internet. We can upload something on the iPhone and send it in. I have clients in Spain, London, Florida, and New York and it's worked for them and you can continue your life wherever it may be.

On the other hand, at certain times it's very nice for the young actor to come into town for two to three weeks and meet people person-to-person. It is 100% going to make a big difference. You just have to have more patience when you live out of town. People have different financial situations and some are able to go back and forth. I would never say that you have to do it, but if you can afford to, it would give you better odds. You do have to find the right team that's willing to do that and it isn't for everybody.

LL: Is there anything you do to help actors get more auditions or callbacks and bookings?

BL: Absolutely YES. There have been times when I have definitely been able to help push it forward faster than the norm. Dressing them, shopping with them, I've met them at the mall, gone to get their haircuts with them. I've gone to acting classes to make sure they are making good choices and watched auditions fifteen times over. Yes, every single thing I have done is to help them. I have called in favors to dentists and dermatologists. I have called friends who are producing a film and said "Linda is perfect for this…." I'll give them certain notes, I've tried to creatively give what I think will work and be more natural. I think that I was right in a lot of cases, so I would say in general, I have a good gut feeling/vibe to what would work.

LL: Do you have any advice to young actors who are just starting this journey?

BL: That it's going to be a long one. There are going to be a lot of bumps along the way. I always say it is how you get through the journey—even going into audition rooms with awful people who pretend to be your friends and then turn around and say bad things. Even if you look back at history in the 40's and 50's, it was the same then as it is now. It was competitive, people weren't always nice to each other. They can do naughty little things that try to derail you and send you back to where you are from—go back to Wisconsin. Don't believe it, don't buy into it. For all those bad, there are so many great people out there. If you really are pursuing it and it's your lifelong dream, you've got to stay on it.

I think it's more about going through the journey—you have to stay in the game—it's not going to be an overnight success. Very rarely; those are one in a million. I tend to say it's a four year plan.

LL: Can you tell me about any actor's careers you developed who then became stars?

BL: Leonardo DiCaprio was around thirteen, fourteen years old and he came to me by default. He had been signed with an agent at the company who left very shortly after Leo signed on. So Leo became my client. He had done nothing; he had only been with the agency for about two weeks. So I got lucky and inherited him. I could tell he was going to have a big career, I just loved him. Yet, his early years in acting were a struggle. He did not come out of the gate busting through; he worked his butt off, and still does to this day. I had him all the way through his Academy Award nominations.

LL: When you inherited him, did you know he would be a star?

BL: I did, I did. Zac Efron was another, he was fourteen. He was sent to me by a friend who had an acting class up in San Luis Obispo. I loved everything about him as well. He had a different vibe to him, and needed a lot of work and struggled in the beginning. He booked some jobs, and then eventually he got *High School Musical* which changed his life.

Hilary Swank was from the Seattle area and she was probably fourteen or fifteen years old when I first met her. She was homeless—living out of her car with her mom. They called me with their last ten dollars. Hilary tells the story best, her mom was making calls from a pay phone in LA, trying to get agents to meet her daughter. They needed to make the appointment right away because this was before cell phones and they didn't have a number where someone could call them back. I was one of the last people that she called and she came in and I fell in love with her deep raspy voice—I couldn't stop listening to her. She was just a bundle of energy. I love her whole family. She immediately started working and then got an apartment. I watched her go through all of her transformations. She was my client until she was twenty years old. I'm really blessed because I'm still close to her and Zac and Leo. I'm fortunate that so many of those around me have been so amazing. It was just my gut reaction to them.

I have these lovely little girls Sophia Grace and Rosie, who are 10 and 6. They got on Ellen's show from the YouTube video their parents posted. I have had a great deal of success with them, from acting to merchandising to mobile apps to game apps to book deals—it's just crazy. The amount of success they have had already is unbelievable.

LL: Any major advice for someone starting out:

BL: Just make good choices. People do naughty things that come back to haunt them. You have to be so careful—this business is really small—as big as Hollywood sounds, it's really small. We have known the same people for twenty-five years. I always tell people, most of the things you are going to say in or outside of that room, you think the door is closed, but there is always someone listening. I've had it where a receptionist called me and said "We heard this… or did you believe they said this, or did this?" Those things will come back to haunt you. Even in who you date and who you hang out with, or the people you surround yourself with . Try not to put yourself in bad situations. You have to know how to handle yourself. Make good choices—that's really important!

Chapter

8

WORKING WITH AN AGENT OR MANAGER

Okay, hopefully congratulations are in order and you got yourself an Agent or Manager. What happens next?

You will come into the agency or manager's office and meet their team. This can include other agents and assistants. It is usually the assistant who gives out the appointments for the auditions. Hopefully, you will be talking to them fairly regularly. Be sure to be friendly to everyone you meet.

The first step would be signing contracts from the Agency or Management Company. Review the contract so you understand what agreements you are making and ask questions if needed. Know how many years you will be under contract with the Agent or Manager, what percentage they will be getting and any other relevant information. Once your contract is signed, be sure to get a copy for your own files. Be sure to know or ask about the procedure that it takes to get paid when you work.

The next step is putting your headshot and resume online under your Agent or Manager's account. They will help you set this up; these days everything is done electronically. However, you still need a hard copy of your pictures and resume when going to auditions. There is a company called Breakdown Services. Every single day, the Casting Directors send out descriptions of characters for the shows (includes TV, Film, Theater, Commercials, etc.) they are casting. Breakdown Services puts these lists together and sends them to Agents and Managers to submit their clients for the roles being sought. Agents and Managers pay a substantial fee to subscribe to this service and sign an agreement as part of their subscription not to give the lists to actors.

Everyday this information is put online to the industry professionals who have subscribed and Agents and Managers go through the list and, via the website, submit their clients that they feel are appropriate for the roles. There are also other companies that put out casting notices. These are not part of Breakdown Services but can be viewed by Agents, Managers and actors. Such as LA Casting and Casting Frontier which handles a lot of commercials, and the other outlets that we have mentioned in previous chapters.

Once your representation has submitted you, the Casting Director will look at these submissions online and decide who they are going to bring in to read for the roles being cast. Just an idea to let you know how competitive this market is, I was looking for a girl in her early twenties for a guest starring role on a television series I was casting, and received over two thousand submissions. This is typical and gives you some idea of how many young people have come to Los Angeles with the same dream you may have.

Now, when the descriptions get more specific or request a specialty, like the actor needs to be able to tap dance or do gymnastics, of course the number of submissions go down considerably. But once you get the chance to audition, you definitely want to make the most of it.

If you have a conflict and are going out of town at that time, make sure you let your representation know so that they don't submit you for something you aren't available to do. Nothing upsets Casting Directors and Agents more than when a client is wanted for a job or an audition, only to find out at the last minute that they are unavailable. It is unprofessional and can have repercussions with the Casting Director and your representation.

A CASTING DIRECTOR WANTS TO SEE YOU:

Yea! Now what do you do? You will get a call from the Agent or Manager or their assistant, giving you all the specifics of your appointment. This includes the time, place and the breakdown of the character and where to get the <u>sides</u>. Your representation will either get them for you through **http://www.sidesexpress.com** or you can get them from Showfax at **http://www.showfax.com**. There is a fee of $68 per year and you have unlimited downloading access for any sides. Otherwise, it is $1.00 a page. Go to the Showfax website for more information on how to sign up.

Now you have downloaded the sides and your work begins. See the following chapters on Auditioning on how to make the most of your auditions.

Breakdown Services is a website that describes itself as follows:

"Breakdown Services, Ltd. is the communications network and casting system that provides the most professional means to reach talent agents and managers when casting a project."

At the online store, **http://www.breakdownservices.com/store,** you can purchase subscriptions to directories of Casting Directors for New York and LA.

The breakdown includes a description of the character that we are looking for, (which includes the age, the ethnicity, some physical attributes, and other characteristics). The size of the role will be listed next to the description, whether it is a Lead, series regular, co-star, etc. It will also include where and when it is going to be shooting. What the project is; a film, television pilot, episodic, internet projects, commercial, or theater. The Producer, Director, production company, network, and Casting Director will also be listed on the breakdown. Sometimes the breakdown will also include a storyline of the overall project.

Here's a typical breakdown that we have put out through Breakdown Services for a couple of past projects. This is what your Agent or Manager will see as they search for roles they can submit you for:

breakdownexpress

Mostly Ghostly (based on R.L. Styne's book) Feature Film Mostly Ghostly Productions SAG	Producer: Director: Casting Dir: Lisa London/Catherine Stroud Casting Asst.: Location: LA or Oregon Start Date: April 7th
SUBMIT ELECTRONICALLY PLEASE	LONDON/STROUD CASTING

[MAX] 11 to 15, he is lovable, but nerdy, offbeat or could be pudgy. He is the outsider at school and his father thinks he needs to stop fooling around with magic tricks and become more "a jock" like his older brother. When Max sees ghosts who start talking to him, he is afraid to tell anyone because his dad has already threatened to send him to military school. (Lead)

[TARA ROLAND] 10 to 15, she is a smart and likable ghost. She figures out a way for Max to help her and her brother, Nicky, find out what happened to their parents and she will help Max become more popular. (Lead)

[NICKY ROLAND] 11 to 15, he is also a likable, good-looking and hip ghost. He is protective of his sister, Tara. (Lead)

[COLIN DOYLE] Max's older brother, 13 to 17 (could be 18 to play younger). He is athletic, the apple of his dad's eye, but a bully and mean to his brother; he's always getting him into trouble. (Lead)

Storyline: Max is a lot like you, except he has two friendly, but mischievous ghosts, Nicky and Tara living in his bedroom. In the meantime, Max is having it tough: his dad wants to send him to boarding school, his brother is a horrible bully, and he is neither cool nor popular. However, Max's life gets soooo much better when Nicky and Tara decide to help him out.

breakdownexpress

SAVING HARMONY Feature Film SAG Low Budget		Executive Producer: Producers: Director: Casting Director: Lisa London/Catherine Stroud Casting Associate: Location: Nashville or Arizona Start Date: Approx. May 14th
SUBMIT ELECTRONICALLY		

[SAMANTHA "SAM" COLTER] Female - Late 30s to early 40s, Caucasian, Southern, beautiful, strong-willed, independent, the ex-wife of country music star Casey Colter. A working class, single mother, burdened by the decaying relationship with her rebellious teenage daughter, struggling with the consequences of past decisions, and confronting the scars reopened after her father's death...LEAD **(STAR NAMES ONLY)**

[HARMONY COLTER] Female - 15 to 16, Caucasian, Southern, modern, beautiful, an aspiring singer/songwriter living in small town Prescott, AZ. Resents her mother, Sam Colter, for trying to control her. Runs away from home and tracks down her estranged father, country music star Casey Colter. At the "Last Chance Ranch", she meets Dylan Stark, one of the programs wayward youths, and finds herself drawn to his devil-may-care attitude...LEAD (PREFER ACTRESS WHO CAN SING AND PLAY GUITAR)

[DYLAN STARK] Male - 16 to 17, Caucasian, Southern, good looking, cocky, a recent arrival at the "Last Chance Ranch". Defies authority from day one. Finds a kindred spirit in Harmony when Casey brings her by the ranch to see her grandfather, ...LEAD

[ARCHIE LLOYD] Male - 7 to 9, cute, insecure, orphaned, the youngest boy at "Last Chance Ranch". Comes to see Dylan as an older brother. Hopes that Sam will be the mother he never had. Finds a soft spot in Casey's heart...SUPPORTING

STORY LINE: In the vein of TENDER MERCIES and CRAZY HEART comes SAVING HARMONY, a multi-generational southern drama about the wounds we carry, and those we leave behind. When legendary music producer JT Grayson passes away, he leaves the "Last Chance Ranch" to his estranged daughter, Samantha "Sam" Colter, a strong-willed single mother. The ranch acts as a juvenile program for troubled young boys, but Sam, already overwhelmed by raising her rebellious daughter, Harmony Colter, puts the ranch up for sale. When Sam reunites with her ex-husband, country star Casey Colter, at her father's wake, she's forced to confront the demons of her past, and choose between the life she's built, and the life she ran away from.

PREPARING FOR YOUR AUDITION

RESEARCH THE PROJECT

Being prepared—which could also be titled "doing your research" can make the difference between a good or bad audition. First you need to know what kind of television show, movie, or theater project you are reading for.

Is it a comedy, musical comedy or drama, thriller, etc.? If it is a comedy, what kind of comedy is it? Is it played more realistic like the show "Modern Family" where the comedy comes more from the circumstances the people are in. Or is it played for the irony (an event or result that is the opposite of what might be expected). For example, in the television show, *The Office*, the entire show is an example of irony, otherwise known as "tongue-in-cheek". Every person does outrageous things and acts like it is totally normal behavior which is what makes the show so funny. In the movie, *The Wizard of Oz*, the Cowardly Lion is an example of irony because we think of lions as being so strong and brave.

Is it more of a broad comedy like the show, *Hannah Montana* or *The Suite Life of Zack and Cody*? Shows that target teens and kids tend to be of a broader comedy style. Some examples of broader comedies: all of the *Ice Age* movies, and most of **Adam Sandler's** movies, such as *Grownups*. Another example would be *Wedding Crashers*, the *Anchorman* movies starring **Will Ferrell**, and the *Austin Powers* movies.

Other types of comedic shows can take a real situation and blow it up out of proportion and that makes it very funny. An example of that would be *Bridesmaids* or many of the skits from *Saturday Night Live* or the movie, *The Hangover*. Or is it a movie like *House Bunny* or *Crazy, Stupid Love* where the comedy comes from the situations people are in?

It is so easy to research a show or a movie because everything is on the internet. You just look it up, research the project and watch it if you have never seen it. The more you know about a project, the better you can do in the audition.

Researching a first time project (a pilot or a movie)

Let's say, it's a first time project like a pilot or a movie that is getting made. How do you research it? You go to the Internet Movie Database at **http://www.imdb.com**. You type in the names of the Producer, the Director, etc. and see what projects they have done before. You can see their list of credits, then pick a couple of the shows and watch them if you are not familiar with their work. If/when you get an audition with one of these people, you will have something to talk to them about and will have a better understanding of their style of work.

This is all part of gaining a real education about the business. The more movies and television shows you watch will give you a better education on what kind of projects you want to act in. You may see an actor or actress that this Director likes to work with and that would inspire you. Or if you are in an acting class you might want to do some of the scenes of actors you admire from watching some of these projects. You get a sense of style of the Producer or Director, the dramatic qualities, comedic qualities, etc. and it gives you an idea of his or her work. For example, here are some Directors who do a lot of projects with young talent: **Steven Spielberg, Judd Apatow**, and **Christopher Columbus**, to name a few. Go to the internet and check out your favorite Directors and Producers. Who do you like?

Also, research who the Casting Director is. You can see if they tend to do a certain type of project or work with certain types of Directors and Producers. As a Casting Director, one of my specialties is to cast projects where my partner and I search and find new talent. Many big stars of today had one of their first breaks with us, such as **Selena Gomez, Miley Cyrus, Emma Stone**, and **Jonah Hill**, to name a few.

The more you know about a show's style, the better an audition you can give. If you have never seen a Director's or Producer's television series or body of work and you go on the audition, that's showing a lack of research and effort. I can't say it enough; **The more you know about the show or film, the more it enables you to do a better audition and be a more well-informed actor.**

I know many examples where successful actors came in super-prepared and nailed the audition. I've also seen others, who, having never even seen the show, come in and just wing it. The ill-prepared auditions are almost never as effective.

Even when auditioning for commercials, know what the product is—research it. Look up the product name online. Know, in advance, who is casting it. Is it a product you want to be representing and have your face associated with?

Also, doing your research gives you something to talk about with the Casting Director, Producers, and Director when you audition. For example, do you have an actor friend who was cast by the Casting Director—you could mention that, or do they cast your favorite show or movie? You are looking to find something in common with the person you are talking with. This isn't phony conversation, this is doing your research and using what you have learned to do a better audition.

Character Research

Another part of research is the type of character you are auditioning for. If you are playing a pop star singer, you need to know how pop stars act, dress, etc. What do you do? Research pop stars. Research different ones on the Internet. You look at what they wear, how they act when they sing, etc. Maybe you even go to a concert. This gives you ideas on how the character should be played.

Another example would be if you were going to play a teen who is a bully. How would you do that? Research movies and TV shows that have characters who played bullies. Watch them. Remember bullies at school? How did they act? How did they talk? What kind of attitude did they display? Were they obvious or did they cover their real actions?

You really want to get into the identity of the character you are playing and be that person. The whole idea here is to **DO** enough research to really be able to make solid choices on playing your character.

MAKING CHOICES

It means you have to decide how you are going to play a particular character. Choice means the act of choosing; selection.

This can be used for any auditions that you go on or scenes you have chosen to do in an acting class. This process is the same whether it's for theater, television or a film project.

The first thing to do is understand your script

Read over the scenes that you are going to audition with. Read them over a few times. If you can get a copy of the whole script, then read it, because this will give you lots of information about the story and where your character fits in. If you can't get the script, don't worry, you can get enough information from the scenes and the breakdown (which describes the character and what the Casting Director, Producers, or Director are looking for).

What I tell people is, as you are reading the material, write down on some sticky notes, your first thoughts—your first impressions. You can refer back to these later and might want to put some of them into the scene.

Another important part of reading over the material is making sure that you know what all the words mean in the scene. This includes all the words in the dialogue and in the scene descriptions. Do you know what INT and EXT mean when they are telling where the scene takes place? INT means interior (for example in a house, in a garage, a school, etc.) and EXT means exterior (in a park, at the beach, on a street, outside a house, etc.). If there are words in the dialogue that you don't know the meaning of, look them up in a dictionary and get them defined. If you are at an age where you need your parents help in finding out what the words mean, ask them. But as an actor, you can't convey a concept in an audition and do a good audition if you don't know what the words mean. You will fumble with the words and be stuck on not really knowing what you are saying.

Sometimes, the writers add directions under the character's name or before the dialogue (angry or upset, jokingly, etc). This is the writer's point of view on how the character is acting so it's a good guideline on how to play that emotion. For example, if the character is supposed to be angry, does that mean he has to be yelling and screaming throughout the scene? No, it is your choice on how to play that anger. There are many different faces to anger including sarcasm, a brooding anger, slow simmer, and even a sarcastic laugh can be very biting.

What is the scene about?

Keep it simple, it doesn't have to be complex. Is the scene about a mother/daughter relationship, a friendship, love, or some sort of conflict, school situations, a bully, a con-artist, etc. This is the first thing that you want to determine, what is the scene about?

There could also be an underlying meaning in the scene; what appears to be going on in the scene verses what is really happening?

For example, a teenage daughter is trying to be sweet to her mom and offers her help with setting the table, but the truth is that the teenage daughter wants to go out to a party that night so she is buttering up her mom to let her use the car.

Another scenario is a cute guy who is trying to woo this pretty girl away from her girlfriends at a bonfire, but the actual scene is about him trying to get the girl to hook up with him.

What is, as they say in the business, the arc of the scene?

By this we mean, where does the scene start and where does the scene end up? Every scene has a beginning, middle and end.

For example, in *Romeo and Juliet*, during the balcony scene, Romeo is struggling to climb up the vines to talk to Juliet. The first part of the scene is his difficulty in navigating his footing. Then he gets up there and talks to her, woos her and then he has to get out of there quickly. This scene has a beginning, middle and end and each part has a different emotion that to play.

In the first part of the trilogy of the *Hunger Games*, Katniss is in front of the judges showing her talent with her bow and arrow. In the beginning, they watch her shoot and she misses the entire target. The judges turn away and instead of watching her, they ignore her. For the middle, she shoots again, and this time she hits the bullseye of her target. She looks at the judges to see if they've noticed, which they haven't. She looks perplexed, and when the judges take no notice of her, she changes her attitude completely. For the dramatic end of the scene, she takes out another arrow and shoots it at an apple which is in a roasted pig's mouth on a platter in the middle of the judge's buffet. The arrow strikes perfectly and pulls the apple right out of the pig's mouth and sticks it to the wall, shocking them. She thanks them sarcastically for their consideration and that is the end of the scene.

We can see how her emotions change from wanting approval, to confidence in her abilities, to hostility at being ignored and dismissed.

How do you go about making these choices?

Once you know what the scene is really about, you start figuring out your choices on how to play it. A good way to make a choice is to see if you can relate your own personal experience to that scene. Now, you may be saying that you are young and of course don't have the life experiences that you are being asked to audition for. What to do in this case, is find some aspect of the situation that you can relate to.

You could be asked to do a scene where the character is jealous about being snubbed for a party or a date. Maybe you haven't been on dates yet. How can you relate this to yourself? Think about a time when you didn't get to do something that your older brother, sister, or friend got to do. You wanted to do it badly and were really envious of them. Maybe a good friend received something for Christmas or for their birthday that you really wanted and didn't get. How did that make you feel? This is the emotion to bring to the scene. Recall how mad you got and maybe you couldn't say anything to your friend because it would make you seem jealous, so you covered it up, but underneath you were upset.

If you take the *Romeo and Juliet* balcony scene where Romeo is struggling to climb up the balcony, and you have never climbed a balcony, what do you do? My suggestion is to think of something that you have done that was very hard physically. What emotions did it bring out? Were you angry, frustrated, defeated, or determined? Any of these emotions can be used in this part of the scene.

Before he climbs the balcony, Romeo is yearning for Juliet and Juliet is yearning for him. Have you ever yearned for someone or something? Maybe you haven't been in love yet, but I am sure there have been situations where you really wanted something with all your heart. If you hoped your parents would take you somewhere, or wished your big brother or sister would help you do something. You wanted a toy so badly or that new outfit, etc. You need to bring those emotions to the scene.

When looking over your material, what are the different emotions you can bring to the scene so you aren't playing only one emotion? You definitely need to be careful not to give a "one note" performance during the whole scene because that tends to get boring. If you are supposed to play a scene angry—don't just yell throughout the entire part. Life is not like that. For example, maybe you do yell a little, then be sarcastic, slam a door or cupboard, then give them the silent treatment. It is much better to find different emotions to play throughout the scene because it makes an actor more interesting. Remember to look for opportunities to bring your character to life as the arc of the scene progresses.

Questions you can ask yourself

Have I ever been in this situation? Have I seen someone else in this situation? Is some part of the scene familiar to you in any way? How am I like this character? How am I different from this character? Have I ever reacted in a similar manner even if it was a different situation?

Going back to the example where the guy is trying to woo the pretty girl away from her friends, here are some questions you could ask yourself regarding that situation. Have you gone out with a group of friends, where a cute guy started chatting and pulled you away from the group? Did you go? How did you respond? Later, how did you explain yourself to your girlfriends or the rest of the group? Or were you the girl left behind? How did you feel? As a guy, have you ever felt so bold that you would pull a girl away from her friends? Did you ever do something that even surprised yourself? Has your best friend ever left you in a mall? Did you have a situation where you felt rejected? All of these can be used to find the emotions in the scene.

What is the evaluation of the scene?

Now you have to decide on the evaluation (to find out or decide the value or worth of something) of the scene. In our previous example, when this cute guy comes up to you, is he someone that you have been dreaming about for the past month? Have you been fantasizing about the two of you being crowned prom queen and king? Or is he a geeky guy from your math class? Perhaps you don't want to embarrass him? Is this your dream girl, or a girl that you heard was hot and a good kisser? Are you a Romeo-type guy who always has a word for the ladies or more of the shy, silent type? The evaluation of the scene is up to your creative imagination, but giving it more importance will give you more to play.

Remember how fearful Harry Potter was to meet Lord Voldemort, and how the scene built up with emotion? This was very different than how he would meet Hermione Granger and Ron Weasley. You have to decide how much value there is to this meeting and build from there.

What are the physical actions of this character?

This also opens the door to the physicality (physical actions of everyday life, your behavior) of your character. For example, are you twirling your hair, twisting your hands, looking bored while he is talking to you, putting on lipstick, flirting, trying to see your face in a mirror or a reflected surface so you can check out your hair, etc. These are all physical actions that bring a scene to life and make people want to watch you.

It is important to start being aware of your own behavior so you can bring it to auditions. How many different ways do you walk into your house and greet your family? Do you throw your books on the counter, do you flop down on the couch, do you come in and say hello to your family happily or say it kind of mad because you had a bad day?

Giovanni Ribisi, when he was first starting in his career, auditioned for the role of a grocery store clerk on **Ellen DeGeneres's** series *Ellen*, and played the scene cross-eyed. The Producers had him do it again and play it not cross-eyed and he ended up getting the job. His audition was very memorable because he made a strong choice. Your choice might not be what the Producers or Director desire for the role, but they can see your creativeness and bold choices. This is something that Producers like to see in auditions, but it doesn't mean they won't change it.

Here are some other examples of physical behavior that became a trademark of the character. There was a character on the TV sitcom *Seinfeld*, who had a neighbor, named Kramer. He was very famous for always coming into Jerry Seinfeld's apartment kinda sliding in the door almost like he was being chased. **Jason Earles**, on *Hannah Montana* who played the part of Jackson was very physical in his part—always falling down into things, getting into situations where things fell on top of him, walking into walls, etc. **Heather Morris**, who plays Brittany on *Glee*, plays the ditzy girl. She always looks a bit spaced out and says inappropriate answers innocently which is the trademark of her character. Can you think of some examples of trademarks of characters?

It is up to you to use your creative imagination to create characters the way you want. There is no right or wrong choice. What is important is to make a choice and go for it.

Using props in the scene

Let's discuss using props in scenes as part of making choices. My thoughts on this are that less is more. If the scene calls for being on the phone, it is okay to use your cell phone in the scene. If you are combing your hair in a scene, it's okay to use a brush or comb in the scene. If you are playing a photographer, it is okay to bring a camera into the audition and use it. I recently read some actors who were playing photographers, and I thought that the guys who mimed "air cameras" were distracting compared to the actors who actually brought a camera into the room. Some actors used their phones as the camera. While doing the reading, you are using the prop to enhance your performance, not distract from it.

One cautionary word that I want to mention is, do not let the whole scene become about the props. I have seen actors spend so much time worrying about the gadgets, etc. and picking up the object on a certain line that the acting goes out the window. Props are part of what you deal with when you are on the set filming. Don't get too overburdened worrying about props in an audition.

The importance of choices

You should make choices that are real and appropriate for your age. Bring as much of yourself to the table as possible in the audition. Don't try to be someone else and mimic other people's choices. I have seen actors in the waiting area of the casting office, listen to other actors practicing their lines or listen through the door to what an actor was doing and then change their choice based on what someone else is doing that they think is funnier or better. Not a good decision, because we, as Casting Directors, are looking for what you as an actor bring to the table. What makes you unique is your individuality and creativeness and that is what we are looking for when we are casting. Does it always mean you will get the part? No, because there are many factors that we consider in the casting process. (More on this in Chapter 13) But what is important is that you make a strong, confident choice and feel good about what you did.

A young teenage actor, **Carlos Knight** came in to audition for the Nickelodeon pilot, *Supah Ninjas* when we were looking for the next Chris Tucker. Carlos was so funny and understood comedic timing so well, that he nailed every comedic moment in the scene. He ended up getting a series regular role on the series.

On another show, an actor came in and decided to play his part with a foreign accent. The part didn't call for that accent, but it was a creative choice. The Producer liked it and he ended up getting a guest star role on a series.

I met **Jonah Hill** for a movie I was casting called *Grandma's Boy*. He had shot a scene in *40-Year-Old Virgin*, but the movie had not come out yet. Jonah auditioned for a role and he wasn't quite right for that part, but he was so funny and charming that I told my Producers that they had to find a role for him. When they met him, they loved him and created a part for him in the movie.

I am saying this again to bring my point home, it is up to you to create your choices. Be yourself and use your imagination in an audition, make big, bold choices and be confident in what you decide.

Confidence, a belief or trust in oneself, is a huge part of auditioning.

Believe in yourself!

SCENE WORKSHEET:

On the next page is a short scene that we are giving you as an example of an audition.

Here are some questions that will help you make choices while preparing the scene. Use these questions for any type of scene you audition for or you can come up with your own.

- List some emotions to try with the dialogue

- Have I ever been in that situation?

- Have I seen someone else in that situation?

- Is some part of the scene familiar to you in any way?

- How am I like this character?

- How am I different from this character?

- Do I know someone else who is similar to this character?

- What does he/she do when this kind of situation comes up?

- Have I ever reacted in a similar manner even if it was a different situation?

Margaret: Confident and hard-headed. Standoffish until you get to know her.

Andy: Awkward in a funny way. Not the best with girls but likable.

Margaret walks over to Andy who is waiting in front of the school by himself.

> MARGARET
> That drawing you drew in class
> was pretty creepy.

Andy looks over at her and looks a little startled.

> ANDY
> Yeah well I wasn't done. It would
> have been better if it was done.

> MARGARET
> Why'd you run away from me
> yesterday?

> ANDY
> I was hoping you wouldn't remember
> that.

> MARGARET
> It just happened yesterday. I
> don't forget that easily.

> ANDY
> (awkwardly)
> Yeah.

Andy looks away. Margaret looks away.

> ANDY
> So you're new in town?

> MARGARET

What gave you that idea?

Andy smiles a little and so does Margaret.

                    ANDY
              I'm Andy.

                    MARGARET
              I'm Margaret.

                    ANDY
              So do you like it here?

                    MARGARET
              (sarcastically)
              Yeah I love it. School's
              the best.

Andy laughs. Andy's mom pulls up in front of them.

                    ANDY
              I have to go. See you later?

                    MARGARET
              I'll be around.

COMMERCIAL WORKSHEET:

Choose one or more of the following commercial dialogs and use the various emotions listed here to practice doing the copy. See what applying different emotions to the words can bring out. You never know what emotion you will have to play for an audition so this type of exercise is good practice!

Emotions:

Enthusiastic	Cheerful
Bored	Sad
Angry	Sarcastic
Hopeful	Apathetic

- Why am I looking so good? You would too if you—GOT MILK. With nine essential nutrients… it does a body good!

- Sweet like cherries, tart like lemonade. Good like the biggest bubble ever. Wrigley's Hubba Bubba Bubble Gum—like Wow!

- A girl can never have enough Barbies. What do I want for my birthday? A Barbie! What else?

- The cheesy flavor of DORITOS' Nacho flavored chips is hard to resist—DORITOS—they're the CHEESIEST!

- So listen, I was standing by my locker after school and who walks by? The guy/girl of my dreams! Our eyes meet and it was magical. Until I realized the HUGE red dot at the end of my nose! I was horrified! Thanks goodness I found Clearasil Ultra Daily Face Wash! It's like magic in a bottle. I wash my face in the morning and now I have no more surprise breakouts. So get Clearasil, and don't let those little red dots ruin your magical moment.

- The best part of school is lunch. Good thing my mom packs me a good ol' PB and J. With Jiff Peanut Butter, it's so yummy it sticks to the roof of my mouth. You know what they say: "Choosy Mom's choose Jiff!"

GOING TO YOUR AUDITION

THE VALUE OF A GOOD ATTITUDE:

Personal attitude is very important throughout the audition process.

"Attitude: a way of thinking or feeling about someone or something, typically one that is reflected in a person's behavior." —New Oxford American Dictionary

Here are my tips in regards to attitude:

- Have a positive attitude when you come in to audition. A positive attitude doesn't mean acting phony.

- Once you walk into the office, take on the attitude of being a professional—

105

(competent and skillful).

- The more prepared you are, the more confident you will be.

- Kids—mind your manners with your parents; don't have arguments with them in the waiting room. All of this is noticed.

- You are in charge of your own attitude whether it is positive or negative.

- If you allow a bad attitude to come with you into the audition, it will affect your auditioning process.

- Do not have public arguments or fights, physical or verbal, with siblings, parents or others.

If you had a tough day at school or your family was irritated with you for some reason, or your mom is mad because she doesn't think you went over your audition sides enough, you must leave these things outside of the casting office. This is part of becoming a professional. Adults have to go to work even when they are mad, frustrated, upset, tired, etc.

Auditioning is your work! No matter what has happened during the day or what is on your mind, you must leave all that behind so you can be present when auditioning. All the best choices that you have made, will be out the window if you are preoccupied, holding a grudge, slightly out of sorts, or generally upset.

When an actor comes in the room and has a good attitude, (by that I mean someone who is prepared, who is present, who is willing to communicate with me and who is willing to take direction) this gives us, as Casting Directors, hope that you could be the person for the role. You aren't glassy-eyed, spaced out, wishing you were somewhere else.

For example, I was casting a series and an actor came into my office for a co-star role and said to me, "I don't know why my agent submitted me for this, because I don't want to do co-star roles." Bad attitude! I am thinking to myself, "Then why are you wasting my time?"

A bad attitude has lost more jobs than any other one thing, be it acting, directing, producing, or any other kind of job in the world. Check your attitude at the door!

Producers and Directors like to work with people who are not only talented, but have a good attitude. **Adam Sandler** uses a lot of the same actors in his movies, (**Rob Schneider, Allen Covert, David Spade, Kevin James**, etc.). Why? Not only because they are talented, but because they have a good attitude about every project they work on.

Sometimes the Director or Producer will ask me, does the child or parent have a bad attitude, and it can act unfavorably for them. They don't want to be stuck with a child/parent situation that is problematic for days/months/years of production.

Another killer of opportunities and creator of bad attitudes is self-invalidation. What is self-invalidation? It is making less of yourself, putting yourself down, focusing on your faults, thinking you are no good and that you will never meet your goals. This is something that will kill you as an actor or an artist. Sometimes, these ideas that you are no good, these negative thoughts, are things that you have heard from others. For example, you have a relative or friend who thinks you will never make it as an actor. You can't let your family's difficulties or lack of success become your problem. You must keep your dreams separate and not give up based on someone else's failures.

There are many ways to combat this. The most basic solution is to stick to your guns and your belief in yourself. Don't buy into other points of view that are negative. Stick to your passions, your dreams, and your own personal integrity.

There's a wonderful unique actress that has recently come on the scene who has a most interesting story of exactly what I'm talking about. Her name is **Rebel Wilson** and she's from Australia.

Here is her story: Rebel was going to a very prestigious law school, graduated and became a youth ambassador and was stationed in South Africa for a year to spread goodwill across the continent. She got malaria and was put in intensive care. She said that she hallucinated that she was at the Oscars and won. It was so real for her that when she came out of the hospital she said, "I know this is crazy, but I'm going to become an actress!"

She also said that when she told her friends and family of her new path in life they all tried to talk her out of it. She stuck to her guns, came to America, and has taken the Industry by storm—working with stars like **Kristen Wiig, Anna Kendrick,** and **Mark Wahlberg** and really stealing the show at times. She's also starring in her own TV show. This is not a girl who would seem like your typical movie or TV star, but that is exactly what she has become. She has her own unique personality and style. Her perseverance and attitude has propelled her to a successful career.

In my experience, very few actors who don't believe in themselves have made it in this industry. Take a look around you at the successful actors and you will probably observe that they all have a very strong belief in themselves. It can be as simple as that!

"Keep your thoughts positive because your thoughts become your words. Keep your words positive because your words become your behavior. Keep your behavior positive because your behavior becomes your habits. Keep your habits positive because your habits become your values. Keep your values positive because your values become your destiny." —Mahatma Gandhi

Now, if you have gone on a number of auditions and haven't gotten callbacks or haven't gotten a job, treat each audition as a new one, difficult as that may be to do. Don't come into the room thinking, "I never get callbacks," "I don't book jobs," etc. All of these things are negative thoughts and won't help you to get the job.

There is no set number of how many auditions it takes to get a job. Some actors have taken years to book a TV series or a movie that takes off and makes them successful. Some actors will be hired on their first commercial audition. My son went out on his first audition, got a callback and booked his first commercial all in a matter of days. Then he went out on at least twenty more auditions and didn't get any of them. You never know, sometimes, it happens like that. **George Clooney** who couldn't be more successful today, did at least fifteen pilots, some of which went to series, before he got the one show, *ER,* that took off starting his road to success.

Miley Cyrus hadn't done any acting before she auditioned for *Hannah Montana.* She had been on stage singing with her father, **Billy Ray Cyru**s, but had not acted professionally. Miley was 12 ½ years old when she originally auditioned for our casting office for the pilot, *Hannah Montana.* Her attitude was one where she was excited to be auditioning, she was very open, willing to take direction, and was happy to have a shot at the role. Every time she had a callback, she had a good attitude and didn't vary off of that attitude. As Gary Marsh, (President of Disney Channels Worldwide), said, "She was as green as the grass, but something was beaming through her eyes that made us feel like we have to take a shot." We believed in Miley because we saw that she had that "It Factor" and she would be a star. After a number of auditions and callbacks, she booked her first series, *Hannah Montana.*

I know a young actor, **Adam Irigoyen**, who moved here from Miami and went out on a number of movie, TV, and commercial auditions. After many, many auditions, taking a year and half, he booked his first series regular role on the Disney series *Shake it Up.* From the very beginning, he had the persistence, passion and a very good attitude. He was happy to get auditions and worked very hard preparing for them. He had a sign up in his room that said, "I will be on a Disney series," that was his mantra. He believed in himself and through hard work made his dream become a reality.

Your personal attitude towards acting is just as important as your talent.

DRESSING FOR A SUCCESSFUL AUDITION:

How you dress is part of making a choice about your character. The idea on what to wear for an audition is to give a hint of the character you are playing. Clothing for the audition is up to you, but it can help to get into the character. Many actors will say that they actually helped "find" their character by putting on a hat or coat or a certain kind of shoes. There was a famous actor, **Peter Falk**, who had a very successful TV series called *Columbo*. He was an unusual detective who always wore this disheveled raincoat and solved murders in a very funny offhand way. The disheveled raincoat was part of his character, just as performing in outlandish outfits has become a signature for **Lady Gaga**. It definitely sets her apart from the others.

If you are playing a runaway, you want to come in the room looking a little ragged—definitely not looking collegiate, and not wearing your best clothes and jewelry. Does that mean if one is playing a super hero, should you come into the room wearing a cape? The answer is No—please.

First know what time period the show or movie takes place in. Are you playing something from a different era? Is this show a western, is it science fiction, or something that is current? Are you playing a bully, America's sweetheart, the girl next door, the nerd, the best friend, the jock, or the annoying sister or brother? Does the character call for a hat, a piece of jewelry, shoes (high-heels, flip flops or boots), eye glasses, etc? Sometimes a small addition to your look or a particular article of clothing can portray everything and is enough to get into the character. Other times, everyday clothes are fine.

If you are playing the hot girl at fourteen years old, don't come into the room with your breasts exposed, and shorts or skirts that are way too short. Dress appropriately for what the role is without going completely over the top because it can be distracting when you are auditioning. I have sat in sessions when the teenage girls or even young women over twenty, were dressed way too provocatively (trashy) and no one paid any attention to their audition. To be honest, they were dismissed because of it. Don't sabotage yourself by how you dress for the audition.

Here are some DOs:

- Dress with a hint of the character you will be playing

- Dress appropriately (age-wise especially)

- Be comfortable in your outfit

Here are some DON'Ts:

- Don't wear so much make-up that you look fake.

- Don't wear tons of jewelry or accessories that will distract from your performance.

- Don't wear heavy perfume, cologne or scented oils because this can be offensive and some people are allergic to scents!

- Don't go out and rent a costume for an audition. This is unnecessary.

- Don't come in like Lady Gaga or if you are a guy, don't come in dressed up like Prince. There will be plenty of time to get dressed up after you get the part, or you may be asked to get more creative at your call-back!

Once again, I will reiterate the word, "hint" of the character. Leave the main make-up and wardrobe department choices to the professionals on the set after you get the role.

Another important part of this is being comfortable in your clothes. If your mom wants you to wear something that you hate—you aren't going to be comfortable or happy about it. My suggestion is to find something else to wear, you are the one coming in the room and auditioning and need to be happy with how you look.

WHAT TO BRING TO THE AUDITION

Sides - (these are the scenes that you read from the script). They would come from the casting office or the agent will give you the code to download them from the internet. When you get an audition for a commercial, the sides sometimes will be given to you when you get to the audition and not beforehand.

Headshot/Resume -Always, always, always bring a few extra headshots and resumes to auditions. You never know when you might need them. Keep a couple extras in the car because it is the easiest thing in the world to forget.

Directions - to the Casting, Agent, Managers, Producer, Director's office.

Highlighters - Bring highlighters to mark your sides if you don't get them ahead of time. Bring a pen or pencil to make notes on your sides if needed.

Agent information - name of your Agent and the agency name (phone # of your agent or manager in case you get lost). Have this information readily available when you go to auditions.

Bring your creativity, confidence, and good attitude. All of the above are part of being prepared which will help you to do better in your audition.

Be on time for your audition. It is even better to be early. Now, I know there are unforeseen circumstances where sometimes you end up being late, but it is better to be early or on time. The reason for this is so you come to the audition not stressed out about being late. If you get there early, this gives you time to go over your sides, to take a few minutes to compose yourself, reaffirm your confidence, and ensure your attitude is good when you get called into the room.

Also, in major cities you can check **www.sigalert.com** or **Google Maps** on your smartphone for your city and see how the traffic looks for the area you are going. This can really save you on wasting time sitting in your car. If you can go an alternative route, it can be really helpful.

Always try and call if you're going to be late to make sure that the casting session isn't over. Call your Agent or Manager and have them call the casting office. This is common courtesy and it is very helpful to casting. Because if you just don't show up, it's considered very inconsiderate and might impair your reputation for being brought in again by this casting office. There is also the chance that we could have filled your spot with another actor. The office will almost always try to work it out for you to come at another time. Casting commercials and television episodic shows are done very quickly so you might not always get another chance to audition if you miss the appointment.

Be patient and courteous while you are waiting because there are also unforeseen circumstances that happen where the Casting Director gets behind in his/or her auditions. Producers could be calling with last minute changes or a deal has to be closed right away. Don't get upset and say when you come into the room, "I waited for thirty minutes" because that shows a bad attitude and can not only throw your audition off, but can make the Casting Director uncomfortable which you do not want to do.

Furthermore, it is good manners and etiquette for you to send the Casting Director and/or the Casting Assistant a note thanking them for seeing you. It can be short but memorable. You can ask for and get the office email, but a handwritten note is always noticed. This is a good place to use those photo postcards that you got made as a thank you note. If you keep good records of the auditions you have gone on, the information makes it easy to know where to send a thank you note. This information can also be easily accessed if you are in a show or a showcase and want to invite industry people.

What do you do when you GO to the audition:

When you walk in the room or just outside the door you will find a Theatrical or Commercial Sign-In Sheet for you to use.

The examples shown above are SAG standard Sign-In sheets. Not all Casting Directors use these exact forms, but probably one similar to it. The one thing that I would suggest, is NOT to fill in your Social Security # on any sign-in sheets. We don't need this information until you are cast in the role.

Kylend Hetherington is a talented young actor who starred in the Broadway Musical and touring company of *Billy Elliot*. Here is an interview with his Mother, Karon, to share with you their experience of the auditioning process.

Lisa London: What age did Kylend start dance classes? What kind of dance classes was he doing?

Karon Hetherington: Kylend started dance classes when he was four. He started asking to go at least a year before that, but I felt that he was too young. For his first two years, he took tap and acrobatics. Each year, his teachers asked me if I would let him join the competition team. I told them that I didn't feel that a four/five year old should have that kind of pressure on him. When he was six, he started with tap and acrobatics again. One day going into class he did an amazing tap dance around the room and the teacher sent the studio owner to me and she basically begged me to let him compete. I said he could, but just in a couple of dances. That year he did four dances at competition. When it came time for nationals that year, they asked if I would let him also do the group jazz dance. So, he had five dances at nationals. The next year, he started jazz, and when he was eight, we added ballet. From then on, he had more and more dances every year. When we left the studio (at age nine) to move to the ballet school, he was performing fourteen dances per competition. As for other classes, he had never taken any lessons in anything but dance.

LL: Did he always like them?

KH: Kylend always loved his dance classes. He asked for his first tap shoes when he was about two or three. He saw **Arthur Duncan** tap on *The Lawrence Welk Show* one evening on TV and was absolutely mesmerized and started asking to take tap from that moment.

LL: How long did he study before he started auditioning? Was *Billy Elliot* his first professional job?

KH: Ky was nine years old when he first auditioned for *Billy Elliot*. He had taken ballet for a year before he auditioned. His initial training at our competition studio wasn't as advanced as the ballet school. His tapping is very advanced and it comes very easily to him, but ballet was more difficult. *Billy Elliot* was his very first audition.

LL: Did he have an agent?

KH: He did not have an agent for *Billy Elliot*.

LL: How did you guys hear about the audition?

KH: I heard about the audition for *Billy Elliot* on the internet. They advertised open casting calls around the country.

LL: How long was the casting process? How many auditions including the callbacks before he got the role?

KH: Kylend's first audition was in Orlando, FL. The closest place the open calls were coming to us was Chicago, but it was happening the same weekend as one of our competitions. He really was too young to audition (the call said boys between ten and thirteen). Before I made any reservations, I contacted the Casting Director via email and told her a little about Kylend, and said he was only nine and I didn't want to bring him if she wouldn't see him. She asked me to send a photo of him. Within a half hour, she wrote back and asked me to please bring him. Ky had never been on an airplane before, and I had flown once when I was eighteen.

I actually only took him because we felt that if he wanted to be a performer, he should see what auditions were all about. When was he ever going to have a chance to experience a huge Broadway audition? The Casting Director kept him at the audition all day, then asked to speak to me. She said that he was too small, but they wanted to see him again in six months and to keep doing what we were doing. Six months later, we went to New York. The Casting Director again said he was still too small, but she wanted to see him in another six months. Six months later, they had open calls in Detroit. We had decided not to go, because we felt that if they had wanted him, they would have contacted us. But the night before the audition, at the dinner table, we asked Kylend if he wanted to go. He said no. I said, "Look, we've gone to Florida and New York. They're in Detroit tomorrow. It's so much closer, why don't we drive down and give it one more try?" He agreed.

After the audition, the Casting Director asked us to return the next day. At the end of that day, the Casting Director asked us to stay after everyone had gone. She said that she wanted Kylend to fly to New York to meet with Stephen Daldry and Peter Darling, the creators. She would be in touch. Now, I can't remember how many times they flew us to New York for callbacks, maybe five or six. Occasionally they would call and ask us to come again.

One time they flew us to New York for two weeks and brought Kylend's ballet teacher from the ballet school in for the second week. They wanted his teacher to see what was expected of the Billys and to have experience with the *Billy* world. Finally, they called and asked him to come to New York and play the part of Tall Boy in the show, and while he was there, he would train with the Billys. Nine months later, he got the part of Billy. They told him that they wanted him to go out on the tour, but that since he was their first choice, he could choose to stay on Broadway instead. We chose the tour.

LL: Had you as a family discussed beforehand, if he got the role, how you would adapt to going on the road?

KH: We honestly didn't expect anything more to come of it. We hoped, but what were the chances? However, we kind of just knew that if anything came of it, we would adapt. We weren't going to start and not finish.

LL: Any other interesting stories you can tell me in relation to Ky getting cast in the role?

KH: The only thing I could add is that Kylend knew he wanted to dance when he saw **Arthur Duncan** tap on TV. Since then, he has met and become friends with **Arthur Duncan.** He has been very lucky and is thankful for everything that's happened to him.

LL: Did he always want to be an actor or only a dancer?

KH: He had never even considered acting. Dance was everything in his life and that's what we assumed he would do. Now, he loves acting as much as or more than dancing.

WORKSHEET

Use this checklist to stay organized for your auditions.

CHECKLIST FOR AUDITIONS:

Date of Audition: _____

Name of Project : _____

Casting Director: _____

Audition Address: _____

Phone #: _____

I HAVE WITH ME:

☐ Headshots & Resume (stapled together)

☐ Sides (mostly for theatrical auditions)

☐ Address & Directions

☐ Highlighter & Pens

☐ Agent/Manager Information

☐ Clothing and Shoe Sizes

DELIVERING YOUR AUDITION

The audition starts from the moment you walk in the door. When you come into the waiting room of the casting office, Producer, or Director, network, or studio office, you need to walk in as a professional.

By this we mean, you are there to audition and not there for playtime or social hour. If you have a few minutes before you are called, go over your lines and really concentrate on your choices.

I have noticed in the waiting room, Actors being very social and talking with each other and not preparing. This doesn't mean you can't be friendly and say hi to someone you know, but your focus shouldn't be on others.

Other reasons why you shouldn't to be having conversations with others while you are waiting for your audition is:

- It can be distracting to you.

- It can be distracting to others.

- You can psych yourself out of the part by listening to other people practicing their auditions and thinking their choice is better than yours.

- Do not become self-conscious because you don't look like everyone else in the room who are up for the same role.

- You might think, "oh I know her" and she is so much more right for the role than me, she has so many more credits, she always gets the roles over me, etc. These are symptoms of a bad attitude and will sabotage your creative choices right then and there, so don't do this to yourself. This is self-invalidation in all its glory!

- It is very enticing to see what choices others have made for the part and to think their choices are better than yours. Self-doubt is more prevalent than the common cold. What happens at that point is, you go into the audition with a couple of choices (yours and theirs) that don't work together. Then your audition is blown because you didn't do what you planned and had rehearsed.

We are looking for individuality and uniqueness. We're not looking for you to be or do the same as everyone else. Sometimes casting sessions are about exploring other options (not the obvious choice) so stay confident, and show them how YOU would do the role. Because you never know when the not-so-obvious choice fits the role better or when that actor surprises everyone in the room with their creativity and they get the job.

I also suggest, do not bring your pets, other siblings, or non-auditioning kids to the appointments. It is an unspoken rule that only one parent comes to the audition and accompanies the actor on the set. If this presents a difficulty to your family, it is important that you find some solution. This also really helps keep you distraction-free to focus on your choices.

WALKING INTO THE ROOM FOR THE AUDITION

This may seem like a "no-brainer", but so many actors walk into the casting office with the wrong attitude. It is very important to walk into the room, look everyone in the eye, say hello, give them a smile and be confident. Instead, sometimes actors walk into the room, embarrassed, shy, fearful, nervous, and act as if they are going to the judge for having done something wrong, instead of feeling happy and confident that they are prepared for their audition and plan to get the job.

When actors come in the room, apologizing for not being fully prepared, (I just got the sides, I had four other auditions today so I didn't have time to completely prepare for this, I just got this audition from my Agent) all excuses that the actor might think would help them in some way to apologize for not being prepared, actually work against them.

A famed acting teacher wrote, "…what I'm saying is that some actors, less talented than others, work more. Usually the reason they work more is because they have a better attitude. They don't apologize."

Whether spoken or not, Casting Directors, Directors, and Producers pick up on this attitude and it is not helpful. Just the other day, I was casting a guest star role on a series and the scene was a very emotional scene. The actress looked great for the role, but she couldn't get there emotionally. I asked her to repeat the scene a number of times and then she stopped in the middle of the audition and told me, "I am sorry, I just can't do this. I can't get to where I need to be." She talked herself right out of that part by apologizing.

Too many actors think that the Casting Director is not their friend, but in reality, we want you to do a good job. Believe me, as an actor, the Casting Director can be a very good friend to you. If you come in and do a great audition, you are solving a problem for us. This helps because we want to find the right person for the role. When meeting the Producers and Director, if you do a great job, you make us look good.

When an actor comes in the room and can't meet the Director's eye, that isn't a good beginning. Even if you don't feel confident and are nervous or scared, be a professional and make this your moment to shine. My friend always says, "Positive thoughts bring on positive reactions." How true that is! I can't say it enough. If you come into the audition feeling confident about your choices, then you'll be better prepared as an actor. If you are nervous, just use that energy and emotion in your scene - don't apologize for it! I often tell actors when they say, "I'm so nervous…" I tell them, "You don't need to be, just go for it".

This is where doing your research and making strong choices will help you to be confident when you walk into the room for the audition.

SLATING/READING FOR THE ROLE

"Slating" is the act of introducing yourself at an audition. Most all auditions are put on camera these days, so feeling comfortable with the camera is an important skill to have and develop. This includes pre-reads and callbacks. Sometimes the Casting Assistants will tape the auditions and show them to the Casting Director. They are also shown to the Producers and Directors. There are many on-camera classes these days that can help prepare you to be comfortable in front of the camera.

Sometimes you will get a call and be asked to film your audition and send a link to the Casting Director, Agent, Producer or even the Director. This is becoming more and more common as we merge into this social media age. You may even be asked to Skype or Facetime your audition with the Director. If you are concerned with getting the best quality for your audition, you can always call your local radio or news station or a small production company in your area. Many of them have video production capabilities and will be happy to help you out. Check if they have a studio and maybe even some lighting to make you look your best. They might help you link your audition to where it needs to go if you are technologically challenged, or your agent or manager can also assist you. But these are skills you will need to develop.

SLATING:

First thing you will be asked to do is state your name and if you are under eighteen years old, you will be asked to include your age. The camera operator might say, "Rolling" or point to you and then you look directly into the camera and with confidence say your name and age. Do not look away, down, off to the left or right; just look into the camera. You usually will be told whom you are reading with. If the Casting Director doesn't mention it before you start, make sure to ask who is reading with you so you know where to direct your attention. When starting your audition, make eye contact with that person. Do not play the scene into the camera unless otherwise directed to do so. It is very important that you always play the scene to the reader whether it is the Casting Director, the Casting Assistant, or another actor. No matter who is reading with you, don't let it influence your choices. Sometimes you will have to read with someone who is literally just reading the part and putting nothing into it, so you have to be focused, stick to the choices you've made and stay true to yourself as an actor.

What I suggest to actors is to know your lines well enough that you can take direction and react to what the other person is saying without looking at the sides or the script. You can hold the sides in your hand and refer to them if you need to. But when getting to the callback stage, you should know the lines without needing them in your hands.

Part of acting is reacting, so while auditioning, it is very important that when you are not speaking, you stay in the moment of the scene and react to what the other person is saying. You don't want to be looking away, fidgeting or trying to figure out what the next line is. Prepare yourself well, know your lines and be the character in the scene.

If you feel that you didn't do what you prepared in the audition, ask to do the scene again. But when doing this, make sure that you change it up and don't do what you did the first time. I can't tell you how many times an actor has requested, "Can I do that again?" and did the reading exactly the same as the first time.

If you feel you flubbed some line in the middle, either keep going and don't worry about it or ask to start the scene over if messing up the line throws you off. I always try and give actors a second chance to do a scene if they feel they messed it up. But not everyone is willing to do this or has the time. That is why it is important to come in prepared and focused!

TAKING DIRECTION

The ability to take directions and change what you are doing is a huge benefit to an actor and can make the difference between getting the job or not.

You may be asked to take new directions on any audition, from the very first one, to the audition that gets you the job with Producers or all the Studio Executives watching. Here are the different types of auditions that one might be asked to come in for:

Pre-read Sessions—this is where you read for the Casting Director or the Casting Associate. This usually occurs for the first audition so that the Casting Director can make choices on who they would like the Director and/or Producers to see.

Callback Sessions—This is for the Producer and/or Director where the Casting Director is bringing their choices to them. This process can go on several times and it is not unusual for an actor to audition four or five times for a role depending on what it is. If you are reading for a role in a movie, a television pilot, a series, a play or any kind of production, you probably would come back a number of times.

Studio Test—This is where you are very close to getting the job and are going to audition before the Studio Executives. This could be for a movie or a television show. You might also be asked to read with another actor at this point as part of a chemistry test. This is where you will be asked to mix and match with other actors so that the Producers, Directors, Studio and Network Executives can see who has the best chemistry together for the television show or film. They are looking to see if it's realistic that all these different people look like they could fit together. A good example of this is the show *Modern Family.*

<u>Network Test</u>—This is where you are also close to getting the job and are going to audition before the Network Executives. (For example at CBS, NBC, ABC, FOX, HBO, Showtime, any Cable network, Netflix, Amazon Studios, etc.)

I have been in many Producer and Director sessions where going into it, I think a specific actor is going to get the job, only to have another actor come in, really respond to the direction that is given to them, and grab the role. These actors have the ability to actually change in front of your eyes. Being pliable as an actor is important because you want to be able to change and take the new direction. They are given the direction (for example: to play the scene with more anger, to pause an extra second for comedic effect, to be more likeable, to cry, etc.) To be able to move within your emotions and still make it real, this is the talent of an actor. Using different emotions and possessing the ability to use your body in different ways are part of an actor's tools. They can be instinctual, but they can also be learned.

I have seen it too many times where the Producer or Director will give the actor a new direction, but the actor isn't really listening and processing what they were asked to do. Many actors lose the job because they didn't make the change to the character and take the new directions being asked.

If you don't understand a piece of direction, ask before doing the reading again. Whether an actor can take direction and change his performance gives the Director some insight into how the actor will be to work with when he gets the job. It can make all the difference in the world. I have seen this over and over again; **one of the main reasons actors don't get cast is because they can't take direction.**

It is very important to be gracious and receptive when receiving direction. Please don't make excuses or try to explain your choice. Just listen, be open and easy to direct.

Once during a seminar I was giving, a young actress asked a very interesting question. She said, "If you give an actor direction, does that mean you like them?" I told her that there are three reasons why I give directions. The first is that I actually like their choices, but I feel I can tweak their performance and make it even better. The second reason is to see if an actor can actually change it up and make it different. This is one of the reasons Director's give direction; to see if actors can change and be directed. Like I said earlier, it is important to be pliable as an actor. The third reason is, sometimes I have seen an actor who is really off the mark in their choices. I give them some new direction to see if they can make it more of what we're looking for. Sometimes this works and sometimes it doesn't.

Now you have read over your script, made your artistic choices, dressed for the role, walked in the room with confidence, so what happens next?

You have said hello to the Producers, Director, or whoever is in the room, with a smile because you are glad to be there. We might ask some questions before you start the audition or you may have a question or comment for the people in the room. This is your opportunity to show your personality to those present. For example, the Producers might ask where you go to school or what are your hobbies. Take this time to show them, you have done your research. This can be the time to mention how you love the Directors, Casting Director, or the Producers work (this is only if you really do love something he or she did). I never suggest to be phony or make up something that isn't true for you. You can talk about a funny story that happened. Keep it short, but Producers like to get a sense of who you are when they are casting the role.

Sometimes there will not be a lot of small talk at the top of the audition. They will just say, "Do you have any questions" and if you don't, then start the audition. If there is a question, now is the time to ask. Keep it simple because if you have made a strong choice, you don't want to throw out a question that the answer will sabotage your audition and confuse you.

When auditioning for a very emotional scene, it is totally acceptable to ask the people in the room if it is okay to read first and then chat. As an actor, you want to be able to sustain your emotions and acting choices and if you need to read before chatting, you can totally do that.

Another point of direction is that if the scene is a very emotional one and for example, you are crying in the scene, please refrain from putting your hands over your eyes or across your face. This comes off like you are hiding and we want to see the emotion in your face. Be aware that you are also on camera and by putting your head down, we won't be able to see that emotion. When the Director looks at this tape later, all he/she will see of your performance is your voice and the top of your head.

It is not unusual for a Director to want to discuss your character. If you are auditioning for a very meaty part and have made some very specific choices, it is possible that the

Director will have a different vision. Be open and flexible and also willing to have a discussion about this. Sometimes, the Director might not have thought of the character the way you have and he will be open to going with that choice. Other times, the Director has such a specific vision, that he will want to do it his way. The Director and actor should have a very collaborative relationship. Some Directors will want to try rehearsing a number of different ways, including your choice. Other Directors love to improvise on a set and end up using some of those moments in the movie. But no matter what, don't be combative with the Director and think that your choice is the only one.

I love seeing an actor take direction and make bold choices. Nothing gives me greater satisfaction then helping nurture talent to do the best they can in the audition process. I remember when I was casting, *The Suite Life of Zack and Cody*, and we were looking for the role of the bellman. I read this very funny and talented actor, **Adrian R'Mante**. I gave him a couple of tweaks to his audition when he read for me. He came for a callback for the Producers and they loved him. What was supposed to be one or two episodes on the series turned into a three-year recurring role. You just never know how it is going to happen. But it always gives me great pleasure to help any actor realize his potential.

As a Casting Director, we have an inside track to what the Producers and Directors are looking for because we have discussed the role with them. We have also seen what works and doesn't work in the auditions, so heed our advice when we give it to you because we only have your best interest at heart.

Here's an interview with longtime Director, **Rich Correll,** who I worked with on the series *The Suite Life of Zack and Cody* and many other shows. Rich has been a Director for so many of the huge hits on television, such as *Family Matters*, *That's So Raven* and *Hannah Montana,* to just name a few. He's worked with many young talents and seen them grow as actors into the stars they are today.

Lisa London: You've worked with tons of kids on your different shows over the years, what do you look for when deciding who you are going to cast for the role?

Rich Correll: The first thing I look for is how is the kid in real life? What kind of kid is this person? Is he or she vivacious? I always talk to the kid in the room before I read them when I'm casting. I want to see how they react to me and how they are as real people. When someone comes in who is really nervous or really affected, I can practically guarantee you that that will become part of their performance as well. And it's hard to talk people out of that. I want to see how comfortable they are meeting the Director, and being under a little pressure. So I'm always looking to see who the real person is.

LL: What special qualities stand out for you when you're casting the young performer?

RC: The first thing I'll do is ask them what they like to do. Do they like sports? Do they like to build things? Do they have hobbies? What do they like to do in school? Are they good students? I ask a lot of kids if they are good students. I think some of the best actors are some of the smarter people. Being a really good actor means you can absorb a lot of things by watching.

The best thing about an actor is someone who really pays attention to their surroundings in their life and what they watch in film and television. They go down the street and see a gardener. They say, "How does this guy act?" and then you look at your grandmother and you see, how does she act? Then you look at your eight year old brother and see how does he act? I want you guys to understand that everything around you—you absorb, you learn, and from learning you hone your skills as an actor.

LL: How important is it to you for an actor to be able to take direction?

RC: As far as I'm concerned, it's really important! I want kids around me that can take direction, because I'll read the script and have a picture of what the script and scene is in my mind. If they aren't doing it exactly that way, which is OK at first, I say to them, "You have to be a little more worried, or you have to be a little more nervous, or you have to be a little more enthusiastic." They have to be able to take that direction.

If kids are going to acting classes, that's what they should be learning—direction, adjustments. So they understand what's going on when the Director says I need you to be more energetic, I need you to be sad, they know what that means.

If they're low energy and you ask them for a change and they can't come up much, it's kind of a giveaway that you're not going to get what you want. However, if they have good energy, if you say to someone, be louder, be funnier, be sadder, or whatever it is, bringing them to that perfect level is usually much easier.

LL: Do you think when a kid comes in and they don't hit those comedic moments, they can be taught?

RC: Comedy is the toughest of all. People don't realize how hard it is to be a really good comedian. Kids who look like they could be a love interest, whether it's a girl or a boy, who are still funny, are really, really rare.

Comedy is very subjective. So what I think is funny, may not be funny to them. What I try to do when I read kids, is to see if they're in the ballpark. I think they can be helped if it's physical comedy. If you write a script, and it's got dialogue in it that's funny, you can explain the comedic beats to them and if they don't get it the 2nd or 3rd time, they're probably not going to get it.

LL: How prepared do you like the actor to be when he comes in for their auditions? Should they know the material very well?

RC: I used to be a kid actor myself… I did the same thing the kids do now. I went to the cattle call auditions, read for the Casting Director, got callbacks, whatever it was. And what I would do—this is just me personally—I would come in, read the script, be familiar with the lines, but not so much that I had them memorized and was off book. I think for a Director, and especially if a Producer is in the room, for television, it's more important to know the dialogue the way it's written, then to try and improvise through it all. You have to know the material—look at it once, look at it twice, run it over in your mind, run it over with whoever you're with, your mom or guardian, if you can. Then be familiar enough with it so you can go in the room, still reading off the page but deliver it with expression.

LL: But know it well enough, so that if you give them direction they are not stuck in, "What's my next line?"

RC: I try to make people feel at home because I think reads should be casual. When people talk to each other in real life, it doesn't sound like they're reading a script. They have to sound like they are not reading, but just having a casual conversation.

LL: On the set, what characteristics are helpful to you with young performers? Any Do's or Don'ts?

RC: When people come to set, I encourage them to tell me about their weekend—we have fun. I'm hoping people can be their normal self on set. Once I start directing, and people are getting their **blocking**, they are getting their comedy beats, kids have to pay attention. In sitcom, the first few days of rehearsal you carry your script, you should write down your blocking, so you're not in the middle of a line, and going, "Where am I supposed to go?" because it just messes up the rhythm of everything. As nice as things may be on set, kids have to listen and they have to really pay attention. They are paid professionals, and this is what we expect of them. Paying a lot of attention to what the Director is talking about, where he's telling you to go, and any direction he is giving you—that's essential. You're there to work!

[Blocking is the process of planning where, when, and how actors will move about the stage during a performance.]

LL: Do you have any advice for the parents of young actors?

RC: We've all seen Stage Moms and Dads that drive us crazy. I think parents should absolutely see that the environment is a good environment. That there's nothing offensive about it, the Director and Producers are treating people well, the set is comfortable, there's plenty of food to eat if you're hungry. The set is kind of an extension of your home. We want everybody to have a good time there. They should let the Director direct.

If they are going to coach the kids at night they should be coaching them based on what the Director told them. I've actually turned around to parents and said I need you to help me—because when he goes home tonight, here's what I want this actor to do. You can help if it's the vision of the Director. So if the parent wants to get involved and help the kids on the side, they have to be part of the team. They have to listen to the Director, and they have to understand what the Producer's write, otherwise they are going to get in the way.

Nobody wants the parents to get in the way, and they get in the way a lot sometimes. We never want parents who are living vicariously through these kids—ever. A lot of parents think, "Oh, now my kid is in Show Business, that means now I'm in Show Business! Isn't this great?" No, no, no, not a good idea. It's for the actor that was hired—not the parent living through them.

LL: How do parents balance their child's life on set and at home?

RC: First of all, childhood is an extremely important part of life. Anything you can do as a parent to increase the normality of these kids' lives at home should be done. Young actors who are on set all the time, aren't having a normal childhood. That's the first thing.

The second thing, as a parent to a young actor, you do not want to become a nuisance or a bother, or a problem to the Producer, because it reflects really badly on your kid and you'll probably get your child fired. I don't care who you are, or how big the show is. Because I've seen shows literally cancelled because of bad parents. If they want to throw their weight around and live vicariously through their kid because the kid's the star, they're going to screw up everything, so they cannot be of that mindset.

LL: Have you given someone their start as an actor on a show that went on to be

very successful?

RC: One of the biggest television stars I saw develop was **Jaleel White**. Jaleel (who played Urkel) was sent to me on Season One of *Family Matter*s. He not only was a very good actor, but he was fantastic at baseball, basketball, and he was an all around good athlete. He was the furthest thing from Urkel you could ever imagine. He didn't show up for the audition thinking he was going to be a physical comedian. The show was strictly about the father and his family. The kids were peripheral to the story. I said to Jaleel, we're going to turn you into a twelve-year old **Jerry Lewis**. I said, you're going to do all of these physical things and bang into things and knock into doors. This physical evolution of Urkel came from what we did on stage.

The first scene he ever did was in the school cafeteria where he had a crush on this girl. I had him come in, bump into a wall, knock down a bunch of trays, knock over a food cart, all of these things. Suddenly he got this reputation of being this great physical comedian. Jaleel was a perfect actor for having the enthusiasm needed for this character.

I also did the first pilot that **Rob Lowe** was in called, *Mean Jeans*, that **Garry Marshall** directed. I was on the sound stage for the first episode of *Bosom Buddies* when **Tom Hanks** walked in and nobody knew him. I was the Associate Producer on *Happy Days* when **Robin Williams** was discovered. Robin Williams was so talented that the Director of that show was really afraid that he would upstage everyone on the show. This was when **Henry Winkler** was the biggest star in television.

LL: Any other advice that would be helpful to the young performer?

RC: My main advice to anybody starting out in the business, especially in acting, is never ever take rejection personally. You're choosing a job where rejection is literally the number one thing. You go into an audition and you're rejected all the time. You're too big, too small, too fat too thin, too old, too young, too good looking, not good looking enough—whatever it is. But you can never ever take that personally. Don't give up!

In my opinion, show business is about these five points:

1. You have to have a degree of talent.

If you have no talent of any kind you probably are not going to make it. You have to have a degree of talent of some kind. You don't have to be the most talented with what you're doing, but you do have to have some.

2. You have to believe in your talent.

You have to wake up in the morning and go look in the mirror and say, "I'm as good as that person I saw last night. I can do it. I believe I'm really good." You have to believe in yourself.

3. You have to have timing.

Somehow, you have to be in the right place at the right time and you will get cast. You just have to have timing. But most people, if you look back on your life, you've had good timing with something.

4. The next thing is politics.

You have to have politics. If you know somebody who is in the business or somebody who knows a casting person, a Director, a Producer or Associate Producer, go to them and say, "How can you help me?" Don't be ashamed, it's okay, that's how the business works.

5. The last thing you have to have is LUCK!

If you're the world's most unlucky person, the other four things aren't going to matter.

So it's got to be Talent, Belief in Talent, Timing, Politics and Luck! That goes for everyone, from **Spielberg, George Lucas**… and anyone who says those things didn't matter in their career is not telling you the truth. And if you have those things and you recognize them and you live by that, you'll do fine!

Here is a good example:

Then unknown **Steven Spielberg** rode the Universal tour tram so many times, he realized there was a certain place he could get off the tram and people wouldn't notice if he got back on later. He got off the tram twice, walked around the lot, with no pass—went in and met an editor and got to be friends with the editor. He showed the editor a film he had made, called *Amblin*, which was an eleven-minute movie, and the editor took that film to **Sid Sheinberg** (Head of Universal Studios). The editor said, there's this kid that's been hanging around and makes great movies, you ought to meet him. Sid Sheinberg met Steven, looked at his short film and said we're going to hire you to make one episode of *Night Gallery*. Steven made a great episode and Sid Sheinberg gave him a deal. All because he hopped off the tram, went and met an editor who took him to Sid Sheinberg. Talent, belief in talent, timing, politics luck—there it was! He had the film, he believed in it, he had his timing, his politics and luck. Same thing with every actor, I don't care how big or small they ever were, that's the way it happened. Anyone you can ever think of, that's the way they did it!

LL: Any other dos or don'ts for actors?

RC: What you have to do is absorb everything, because day to day life, from the time you get up out of your bed to the time you go back to you bed, is all about seeing the life experience. You have to absorb it all to be that actor. As far as kids are concerned—start right now. If you come into a casting session and I say you are a great ten year old kid, but I need you go to through this transition of life and you're going to end up as an eighty year old guy. How does an eighty year old guy act? I want to see it.

MAKING YOUR EXIT

Now that you have done your audition and are finished, what do you do now? Usually, the Casting Director will say, "thank you for coming in" or something of that nature. You reply with something like it was great meeting or seeing you again. Make eye contact and walk out of the room as a professional actor with confidence. Do not ask the Casting Director when do you think you might hear about a callback. This puts the Casting Director on the spot and sometimes we don't know because we have to see all the actors that are auditioning for the role first. You don't say, "How did I do?" This doesn't show confidence or professionalism.

Leave with a good feeling about what you did. When you leave the room, you're done. Let it go. One of the things that I always tell actors is that when looking back at what you did in the audition, ask, did I do what I planned in the audition? If yes, then move on and let it go because there are many factors that go into casting.

Almost all Casting Directors take notes on each actor for every audition. If you are in doubt about the audition, have your representation call or email for feedback. But be aware, don't bug your representation over and over to get feedback because sometimes the Casting Directors are busy and won't get to it right away. Also, another bit of information is that Casting Directors won't always give specific feedback. They might say, he or she did a good job, but we are going in a different direction or that someone else was a bit stronger for the role. Feedback isn't all that helpful unless you get very specific information which could help in future auditions. I think actors need to rely on their own intuition as to whether they achieved what they wanted in the audition or not.

A girl auditioned for a guest-starring role on a series I was casting and was distracted by the noise coming from the other room where actors were auditioning for another project. Sometimes, there are multiple projects being cast in an audition space. (Unfortunately, we don't always have sound-proof audition rooms.) She was so distracted that she could not deliver her performance. I gave her a couple of chances to do the reading and she just couldn't concentrate. Her manager then emailed me and said how she apologized and felt bad for what occurred. Apologies don't get you the job! When you are in the audition, be really prepared and stay focused, then when unforeseen things happen, you are able to keep your concentration and perform.

This is the result of what we spoke about in an earlier chapter, "Personal Attitude." Something could happen before you arrive at the audition that was disturbing or distracting, and the result is that it throws your attention and focus off your audition. Life is all around you and things are always happening that may put you off your game. It is up to you to be a Professional. When you walk through the door for your audition, rise to the occasion, put your best foot forward, and perform. Every audition is a performance, so make yours the best it can be.

If you didn't accomplish what you intended when rehearsing because you got nervous, forgot or second guessed yourself in the room and had doubts, then you have to work harder for the next audition. Make stronger choices you can stick to and be even more prepared so as not to get thrown in the audition. Don't get stuck in "Oh my gosh, I blew it." Too many actors get stuck in all the "No's" and you just can't do this to yourself.

Treat every audition as a new one and don't think, "I don't do well in auditions," "I messed up my last audition" or "I never get callbacks." All of these thoughts are negatives and you must let these rejections go. Being a successful actor is all about persistence and you never know when that one audition is going to turn your whole career around. But I can assure you that if these negative thoughts take over, this will not be the audition that turns your career around.

You have to treat each audition as if it could be the "one". Do your research, prepare well and get into the correct frame of mind – these are all signs of a professional. Each audition should be a new exciting chance, where you get to create a character and it is an opportunity to meet new people. Don't take auditions for granted. There is a good chance that the Casting Director or Producer will remember you for another role they are casting, even if you aren't exactly right for the role you auditioned for.

When we were casting the series, *Supah Ninjas*, there was a time when I read a girl for one part but she didn't end up getting that particular role. She made strong choices and we kept her in mind. A few episodes later a different part came up and we brought her into the Producers again and she ended up getting a guest-starring role in a different episode.

For many actors, getting an audition is the goal. Really, this is just your starting point, because the process of auditioning has many steps that are very important to succeeding in being cast in the role. Don't throw the auditions away and don't take them for granted. Take the time to be prepared, and don't let it all "be a blur"—stay in the moment and most of all, enjoy yourself! Because the more you do that, the more everyone in the room will be happy to have met you, and that will always pay off in the long run.

These are my successful tips for auditioning. When applying these steps to your auditions, you should have much success. Happy auditioning!

WHAT HAPPENS WHEN YOU GET THE JOB

Your Agent will negotiate the deal and the production office of the project will usually send contracts to your representation, although sometimes you will receive the contracts on the set. This often depends on whether it is a movie or TV series as to whether it goes to you on set or the Agent first. Sometimes it is just a time factor from when you actually get cast and it starts shooting.

But no matter what, you shouldn't start filming without first signing the contract. Most productions won't let you start without signing the contract. There are many forms to fill out. Make sure you bring your Picture ID or Driver's license or passport to prove you are an American citizen. If you are from another country, for example, Vancouver, Canada, you will need a O-1 Visa or a Green Card.

Once the deal has been closed, you may be asked to have a wardrobe fitting the day before you shoot or even a makeup test if it is something where they have to do elaborate makeup or special effects.

Special Factors If You Are a Minor:

If you are under eighteen years old, you are going to need a couple of extra things before beginning filming. See the next chapter on Legal Requirements for all the information you will need.

For television and film projects, there is a read-through of the script before filming begins. This is where the entire cast, the Director, Producer, Casting Director and other production personnel sit around a very large table and read through the script. This gives the Writers, Director and Producers a chance to hear the lines and decide if they want to make changes to the script. It's a good chance to meet all the players involved and to have the experience of being at a table read and getting a feel for the show.

TIPS FOR BEING ON THE SET:

Have all your lines memorized before you show up for filming. You definitely don't want to be hung up on your lines when you get on the set and start rehearsing and blocking the scenes or having props to deal with.

From the production office or your Agent's office, you will get a call time (your time of expected arrival on the set). When you are on the set, get the production office number and or Assistant Director's number so that you always have a person to contact in case of an emergency or if there is a problem.

You can also ask for a crew contact sheet and make sure you get your call sheet before leaving the set every day. Call sheets are made up of the actor's call times, scenes you are filming and shooting locations. They vary every day, so it is important to make sure to know what time to arrive and where you are filming. The Assistant Director hands the call sheets out at the end of the day, make sure to get yours before you leave. For your first day of shooting, you will receive a phone call the night before from the Assistant Director as to the time and place where you need to report.

Also, make sure you know what scenes you are shooting the following day so that you can be prepared. These things change sometimes at the spur of the moment because of weather, an actor's availability and many other production factors, always stay on top of what scenes you are doing. Make sure you know your lines well and that you really understand your character. It is a rarity that a show shoots a script in chronological order. Sometimes, they even start with the ending and this is why it is important to have made strong choices on your character.

Obviously, the Director will have input on this too. But you got hired because they liked what you did in the audition so make sure not to change everything when you get to the set, without discussing it with the Producer and/or Director.

Sometimes, you will have to wait hours or all day to shoot your scene. Come to the set with things to do that will keep you occupied and make sure you keep yourself fed and rested because you don't want to run out of energy when it comes to filming your scene.

Stay focused on your character also by rehearsing your lines, maybe even practice them with another actor in the scene if the opportunity arises.

Film and television sets are known for having delicious snacks (craft services) and catering. This can be a smorgasbord of delicious cookies, cakes, bagels, fruit, vegetable and dips, cheeses, crackers and drinks. It's easy to over indulge. You definitely want to pace yourself so you don't get groggy while waiting to go on set to film your scenes.

You will be fed either breakfast or lunch. If it is a late shoot, it would include dinner. A word of advice for those kids who love sugar—Don't eat so much sugar that you get super hyper or sluggish and then when they get to your scene, you are not able to perform at the top of your game. Parents, watch your kids to make sure they aren't over-indulging. These things are free, so we tend to want to take advantage of them, but you will be wise to handle this with good judgment.

Don't forget that your parents or a guardian will be with you on the set if you are under eighteen years of age. Always mind your manners with the people who are there assisting you. No prima donna attitudes, and that goes for the parents also!

Show up on time or even be early for your call time. Be friendly with the people you are working with and professional, but most of all have a good time. Take it all in, learn all you can by being on the set and enjoy the experience.

BEHIND THE CASTING DIRECTOR'S DOORS

Many people ask me what goes on in the casting process, why don't I (or my kid) get a callback? The Casting Director said that I did a great job, so why didn't I get the part?

Well, I am going to tell you that there are as many reasons why, as there are people who audition for the part. I will try and give you some insight into some of the reasons so that it takes the mystery out of why my child, teenager, or you, etc., didn't get a callback or book the job.

First of all, there isn't any one simple answer. Everything I have talked about in the earlier chapters of this book, gives you insight into what you need to do to get the most out of your auditions. Are you really prepared, have you done your research, have you made strong choices, do you have the correct attitude, are you acting because it is your passion or someone elses? All of these things are a very important part of the answer.

Here are some other reasons why, though one does a great job, he or she didn't get the part. Say we are trying to match your child with two actors who have been cast as parents in a show. You could do an awesome audition, but another young actor could be a better fit physically. He or she just looks more like he could be part of that particular movie or TV family than you do. You just can't fight that physical thing.

Another situation that comes up only too often is that the Producers or the Network Executives change their mind sometimes after, and even during the creative process. Suddenly we're looking for ethnic choices for the role or a more quirky way to go. Initially we were looking for the more handsome or young leading teen, and now we're looking for a young **Dustin Hoffman**. We can start out looking for an actress with blond hair and then it changes and they really want a brunette for the role or vice-versa.

Maybe you auditioned for a comedy; everyone in the room laughs at all the right moments and appear to love your choices. But, you don't get the part. Maybe you even get a callback and make all the same choices, just like we spoke about. You have more confidence and it all feels great—but you don't get the part. Does that mean because you didn't get the job, you did badly? No! It just means that the decision makers went a different direction with the role, or another actor played it even better.

Now on the other hand, I am going to talk a bit out of school. The reality is that I have auditioned thousands of kids, teens, and adults for different roles over the years. Truth be told that probably about 80%, though they may make us laugh or cry and we may say, "Thank you, nice job." we know that they will not be called back. The reason that they won't be called back could be because their skill level is not up to the standards that we are really looking for, and we don't see their potential at this time. It doesn't mean that it won't develop with more classes, performances and more auditions, but right now, the Casting Director in front of you doesn't see it.

What is the Casting Director looking for in someone who doesn't have a ton of credits? Charisma, talent, and personality are all part of it, but one of the most important things is a person's potential. Do they have the potential to carry a series for a number of years or be the lead in a movie? By this potential I mean, the ability of the actor to really take the directions given to him, make them his own, and use them in the part, and become the star they are looking for. Also, we are looking to see can this actor learn and grow as an artist.

There are also those times when an actor, who doesn't have a ton of experience but has the charisma to come into the room and capture the hearts of everyone, gets the job. It happens sometimes, that even if you don't have a long list of credits, your charm, personality and potential talent, gets you the job.

Just to make it perfectly clear, we may feel certain actors are delightful and even memorable, but we might also feel that they aren't quite ready for the part yet. They aren't prepared enough, don't know how to hit those comedic or dramatic moments. Sometimes it may be that they can't repeat what they did during their auditions, if the Casting Director or Director asks them to do it again or they can't take changes in direction when they are asked to. This is really an important part of the acting process, being able to take a new direction and change from what you originally did.

Keep in mind that this is a collaborative process—between the Casting Director, the Director, the Producer and you, the actor. It's good that you have made some strong choices for your part, were able to bring them to life, and they are appreciated.

Now, when the Director asks if you could bring it up (or down a bit) or change the character and bring in some humor, are you a good enough actor to incorporate these changes in a quick and efficient manner? Do you have a good enough grasp of this character to find a way to bring these new emotions to the audition on the spot? These are the qualities that good actors are made of. It makes a huge difference to the Director and Casting Director to watch the actor make these changes and still remain believable and charming.

Should you take it personally if you didn't get the job, No! Move onto the next audition and treat every single one like it is a new opportunity. Don't get stuck in the rejection. Don't get into the thought process that, on my last audition I did good, but I didn't get the job… therefore, why bother? Each audition should be looked at as a new, fun opportunity.

The silver lining to this feeling of rejection is that every time you do a great job, you are making an impression on that Casting Director, Producer and Director. As I discussed previously, even if you don't get the role and do a memorable performance, we, as Casting Directors, always remember you. Sometimes, it takes several times in front of the Casting Director before you get that callback or the job. But it is always important to do your best and make a good impression because you never know when you might be called back for a different role at a later time.

It's a great feeling to know that you "nailed your audition". You feel it went great, and it probably did, but you still don't get the callback. When your Agent or Manager tells you, you just can't believe it. Many times I may really be rooting for a specific actor, but the Director or Producer have their own favorites. Sometimes, we don't all agree and there can be lengthy discussions on who should get the part. There are many opinions and in the end, sometimes you win the battle and sometimes you don't. But if you did a good job, don't despair, because everyone in the room will have noticed that you were talented. I have even been in the room where the Producer decides that this particular actor, even though they don't get this role, he will say to me I am going to write a different role for them. Or down the road, there is this role coming up and lets bring that actor or actress back for that part.

Another factor that plays into getting an actor a job is the ability to be consistent in your auditions. I can't stress this enough. Recently, in casting a new television series, I was looking for a girl who was in her early twenties, very pretty and very sympathetic. The role required the actress to have a very big emotional range. The actress who ended up getting the job, was consistent in her readings from the very first pre-read with me to the chemistry test with the lead actress she would play opposite. That was one of the discussions that took place with the Producer, how this girl was always present in the audition and always delivered a top-notch performance. This gave the Producers confidence that she could deliver what was needed on the set.

When you are reading for a comedy, it is very important to bring humor to every audition. I have seen it on pilots where a teen will come in and be funny for me and then when they come in for Producers, they can't hit those comedic moments. Sometimes they do it great for the Producers and then lose it for the second or third callback. *Consistency is very important and you need to bring that humor every time.* Especially when you are reading for a series regular role, the powers that be want to know that you will be able to deliver. Your natural instincts need to be sharp when it comes to comedy or a drama. We will even recommend that you see an acting coach to help you make those moments, if we see that your natural instincts are there, but they just need to be fine tuned a bit.

Recently, as I was casting a pilot, we saw a lot of kids who I thought had some potential, but they weren't quite able to nail the scene enough to get cast or called back. We have a wide variety of acting coaches that we send people to help them in finding these moments. From this training, it could increase their chances of getting a callback or booking the job.

Here's another aspect that happens in casting. I may be reading lots of people for the role and there may even be callbacks. Then I come to find out that a relative or friend of the Producer or Director is getting the job. There is no way to prepare or defend this. It happens and it is just part of the business. But even the friend or relative, if they don't deliver when the camera is rolling, and continue to be consistent in their performances, will not continue to get hired.

Also, sometimes we will read actors for a part while at the same time we are trying to get a star or a "name" attached to the project. We will read actors as backup in case we don't get the star the Producers wanted. You might even know that this is taking place. Does that mean you don't come in and give it your all? Of course not! Because like I said before even, if you don't get this role, when you do a fantastic reading, the Producers will possibly consider you for a different role in that or another project.

Now, I want to discuss another aspect of casting. Some actors come in and have the "It Factor". I discussed this before, but I am reiterating it again because from time to time you will hear it. Sometimes, as Casting Directors, we meet people who have this "It Factor". When we first met **Miley Cyrus** and **Selena Gomez**, we saw that they had the "It Factor". **Kerry Washington, Leonardo DiCaprio** have that "It Factor", **Beyonce Knowles**, **Ben Affleck** etc. There are many examples of actors, singers, athletes who have this. I am sure that you can name quite a few if you think about it. If you are a teenager or an adult reading this book, you're probably wondering, Do I have this "It Factor?" As a parent you may be thinking, Does my kid have the "It Factor"? Now that I think about it, every parent probably thinks that their child has the "It Factor." I certainly do, but the question is, does everyone else who meets my child think the same thing? It is the broad perception of this factor that makes it a reality.

It doesn't necessarily mean that you or your child or teen isn't talented if they don't have this "It Factor." They are many people in this industry who don't have this, but they still go on to have wonderful careers and are amazingly talented. You can have a spectacular career without having this characteristic. Also, as one grows as an actor and artist, you gain more skill, your confidence grows and you persist; this factor can potentially come into play.

Katy Perry started out singing gospel rock and the record company she was signed with dissolved. She continued to develop her musical style and worked with several different record labels. She collaborated with many different musicians and evolved into the persona that turned her into a mega star. **Lady Gaga** was always creative and she has this amazing ability to "re-invent herself". She wasn't recognized as a star in the beginning, because she was writing songs for other popular artists at the time, but she believed in herself and her talent and persisted until the world agreed with her.

Daniel Radcliffe and **Emma Watson** from the *Harry Potter* movies have this "It

Factor." **Jennifer Lawrence** from *The Hunger Games,* who just won an Academy Award for *Silver Linings Playbook* at the age of twenty-three, has this characteristic.

The fact that she was obsessed with being an actress, helped to fuel her talent and her confidence. These are some examples of actors and actresses who I think have this quality and apparently others agree with me.

I wouldn't sit and wonder about this "It Factor." Just work hard and persist, if acting is your passion. To be honest, your persistence and passion will take you a lot further than any other reason.

I hope this chapter has given you some insight into what goes on in the casting process and how many different factors come into play when you get a callback or get cast in a role.

PERSONAL ATTITUDE FOR
PARENTS &/OR GUARDIANS

This is relevant to any parent of an actor who has a child or teen under eighteen years of age.

You are there to support your kids. By this we mean to encourage them in their goals, their dreams and their endeavors. As we know, some kids need more support and encouragement than others. For some young aspiring actors, this is going to be a flight of fancy, just like their desire to be a professional ball player or a ballerina. For others, this is going to be a life goal. It is not up to you as parents to decide which it is because kids can surprise you at any turn. Mine certainly do, all the time. It doesn't really matter whether you think they can do this or not. What matters, is what your child thinks. If they believe in themselves and they think they can do this, then as parents, you should support them and let them go for it.

I am not saying that you should pack up your house and move to Los Angeles because your child has said that he wants to be an actor. But help him or her to find local classes, workshops, theater productions that he or she can be involved in. Encourage them to take a drama or musical theater class especially if your school offers that. This will also show if your child is ready to do what it takes to develop his craft.

There comes a time when others are encouraging you to come out to Los Angeles and give it a try. Or you see that your child as an actor, has gone as far as he can go in your city, then you can work out the logistics of coming to Los Angeles. There are different people who can help to figure out a game plan when you decide to come to LA. This could be anyone from a relative, friend, or a Manager or Agent from another city that knows someone here in Los Angeles that can help you learn the ropes.

This takes a lot of work with the entire family to decide if it is the right thing to do. This decision will impact, not just the child who wants the career, but his or her siblings, and the other parent who is staying behind. And of course, there are the finances and the security of leaving your home, friends, and extended family.

Some families come out to Los Angeles just for **pilot season**, which is the time frame between January and April when TV studios create new shows. I'm not saying that pilots only happen during that time, but a large amount of them are cast during that time period.

I would strongly suggest that you exhaust all opportunities in your local city first. This is also a good idea because you can start building your child's resume. This gives your kid the chance to see if they really like acting and what it takes to have a career in the entertainment business. Do they shine when they go on auditions? Do they like meeting new people? Can they memorize lines? Do they love being on stage and performing? The answers to these questions are going to be quite obvious whether this is just a pipe dream or a passion of your child's.

There are life lessons in any choice that one makes and sometimes failure is our best teacher. Better to put oneself out there, than never to have tried at all.

Just like Alfred Lord Tennyson (who was the Poet Laureate of Great Britain and Ireland) says, "It's better to have tried and failed than to live life wondering what would've happened if I hadn't tried."

Another thing to know is that very often when we are doing searches across the country for new talent, we will seek out acting teachers, coaches, agents, or specialty schools if we're looking for a "certain kind of talent" in many different cities. When they have an actor they think fits the role, they put themselves on camera in their hometown, and send it to us so we can view the audition via a link. It all happens very quickly and is quite efficient. We might have you come out to LA for a callback, but this is something we would discuss with you at length. You don't have to "move to Los Angeles" in a blink because your child has said they want to be in movies or on TV.

For the parents who are in the midst of supporting their child/teen's career, here are some of my Dos and Don'ts:

1. Do not argue with your child on the way to the casting office or in the office.

This will put their attention on the argument and they won't be present in the audition.

2. Do be sure that your kids are well-fed and well-rested.

I have found that kids who come to auditions who are well-fed, are more present, more able to follow directions, friendlier and happier overall. From my experience with my own kids, they can be quite ornery when they haven't eaten. Once I have ensured they have had a healthy snack or some protein, they are definitely a pleasure to be around.

If you don't have time to stop for food, bring healthy snacks and water they can have in the car. Do not give your kids sugar that is going to make them bounce off the walls.

Lots of kids are tired by the end of their school day which is a typical time for their auditions. It's okay to have them take a nap, but be sure to wake them up fifteen to thirty minutes before they get to the audition. This is so they can get their energy up before they come in to do the reading.

3. Don't over-rehearse with your child/teen.

If they want to go over the lines with you, that's totally fine. But, we are looking for them to be as natural and real as possible, so let your child's instincts be the guide.

4. Don't direct them to the point where they are so rehearsed that they can't take different direction.

Sometimes kids become so robotic, that when the Casting Director, Producer or Director give them a direction, they can't change it up because they are so stuck in what they were previously doing with the scene.

5. Do keep a good attitude toward the Casting Director, Casting Assistants, etc.

6. Don't let your kids play video games before or during auditions.

I strongly suggest that there be no video games while your child is waiting for his or her audition. Video games tend to scatter a child's attention and it takes their focus off their choices and the audition can suffer in this case.

7. Do decide if the material your child is auditioning for is appropriate for their age.

It is up to parents to look over the material and decide if the language and content of the project that your son or daughter is going to audition for, is something that you are comfortable with. Sometimes, there is an awesome opportunity for your child to be in a film or television series, but the material is not appropriate. It is up to you to decide, and even discuss the project with your child, depending on their age.

Anything that is rated R could be a guideline if your child is under eighteen. It is a tricky decision to balance an artistic opportunity with a show that has questionable values. But there are a lot of great shows on television and movies that deal with dark subjects that have young actors in them and are brilliantly acted.

There have been young actors in film, television and theater dealing with dark or risqué subjects from the beginning of the entertainment industry, and you and your family will have to figure out what is best for their career.

8. Do not force your child to continue acting if he decides at some point that he doesn't want to do it anymore.

This is not an unusual occurrence. It can happen for a number of reasons. One, that they lost their passion for it. Two, that there was too much rejection. Three, they would rather do something else with their free time, like play sports, etc.

This is a hard industry. Just because you child books a job, doesn't necessarily mean they will book the next one. One success doesn't guarantee future successes. But as I said before, if it is their passion, don't give up on a few rejections. It has to be something that they continue to want to do. The beauty of acting is one can do it at any age.

These are safety points from SAG (Screen Actor's Guild) regarding your child and production:

- It is the minor's parent's primary and most important responsibility to ensure the safety of their child.

- The minor or the minor's parent's always has the right to refuse to perform any activity that might be hazardous to the minor, either physically or emotionally.

- If the minor believes the situation is dangerous or is fearful (whether real or imagined) the minor cannot be required to perform.

- Outdoor shoots often require long periods of time in the elements. Parents should guard minors against dehydration, hypothermia and overexposure to the sun. Parents should not hesitate to contact first aid personnel immediately if the minor is too wet, too cold or too tired.

- Parents should consider the impact of mature or emotionally difficult dialogue or actions on their child's well being. Only the parent knows what their child can tolerate and therefore MUST ensure their well-being.

Other information:

Many times Producers and Directors have asked me, do you know anything about the parents or have you talked with them? This is asked especially when it comes to casting kids for series regular roles or on a movie where you are going to be working together for a long time. They want to make sure that the parents are on board and agreeable. Also, that they are going to be able to adapt to changes and that you can communicate with them.

Sometimes you have situations where an actor has to relocate to Los Angeles for example, to do a pilot or TV Series. Often, only one parent will move with the child. Before your kid starts auditioning for out-of-town work, make sure that as a family, everyone is in agreement if your child gets so fortunate as to book a series or movie. These separations can wreck havoc on families.

If you talk about it beforehand then it's not such a shocking decision to relocate for the period of time that the young actor would be working. Otherwise, if there are other children involved and the father (or the mother) has a job they can't leave, it might prohibit the child from auditioning at all. The kid will have to wait until he's a little older (and on his own) before he auditions for something with such permanent ramifications.

For example, I have a friend whose nephew is a very talented young actor. He was little for his age and so he had opportunities to go out for younger roles than his age group. But he lived about ninety miles from Los Angeles. Every time he got an audition, he had to get out of school early, drive down to LA and do the audition. Then they had the joy of sitting on the freeway for the extra hour or so to get back home due to the traffic. After a few months of this, his Mom made the decision that this was just not the best life for him even though he had actually gotten some parts and worked professionally. He had many wonderful opportunities to act within their city and community which he took full advantage of and enjoyed immensely. She just felt it was a better life for him and their family, and kept his acting to those projects. He was fine with it too. He will make the decision in a couple of years if he wants to follow that dream of being a professional actor. Or he will enjoy acting in local shows and community theater, and of course that decision is his to make.

On the other side of the coin, **Gracie Dzienny** who is from Ohio, went on tape for the lead role in the Nickelodeon series, *Supah Ninjas*. Her family was willing to come out to Los Angeles and relocate if the pilot got picked up, which it did. The show filmed in LA for one season and then got moved to Pittsburg to be filmed for the second season. Talk about flexibility! They were willing to go wherever the filming took place.

Obviously, there are labor laws that are followed when hiring kids and there are teachers on the sets to enforce those rules so kids don't work over the amount of hours they are allowed, etc.

As a parent, this is an adventure that can take you to places and experiences you only dreamed of. The opportunities are limitless so my advice is to enjoy the road together. Encourage your child. Be the supportive arm and ear that they need and continue to do whatever it takes to help them reach their goals.

ACHIEVING YOUR GOALS

There are so many stories of young and middle-aged actors living in poverty, sleeping on their friends' couches, ready to buy a ticket back home when all of a sudden, that big break happens for them. How often have I heard the story of people who feel that they can't take the challenge of this lifestyle any longer or they are just about to give up when they agree to give it one more shot and go on that 2,464[th] interview and that is the one that gives them their break and catapults them into the beginning of a career.

Victoria Justice was eleven years old when she came in and auditioned for me for *The Suite Life of Zack and Cody*. This was one of her first auditions and she ended up getting a guest starring role on the show. She then went on to audition for a number of pilots for different networks and didn't get any of them. They were, of course, disappointed. Her mom said that a Studio Executive felt that Victoria wasn't ready yet to carry a series, and they were thinking of moving back home to Florida. I told her that she shouldn't give up and move back because that was only one person's opinion. I strongly encouraged her to stay out in

Los Angeles and I said that within six months, she would be a series regular on a television show. Well, within six months, Victoria was cast as a series regular on Nickelodeon's *Zoey 101* and that led to her own show, *Victorious*. So much for one person's opinion!! This shows that if this is your passion, you must find a way to persist and not give up.

The first good role an actor gets may not even make them into a star, but it puts them on the road of their career path. There may be someone they meet while working on that project or who sees their performance that calls them, and says, "I want you to audition for my next movie or my television show". It may just be that working professionally and being paid, renews their sense of confidence that they can achieve this goal and continue pursuing their passion to be an actor.

This brings me to an important part of the industry. You can't study to be a star. You can study and work on your craft to be an amazingly talented actor. Your focus should be on doing the best job as an actor that you can do. One can't look at a star's path and think, I can do exactly what they did and then I will be a star. Each individual makes their own choices and has their own journey to follow. Make your goals, write down your dreams and follow your own path. The most important part of this path is believing in yourself, working hard, learning everything possible about your craft, and persisting.

Never stop dreaming, never stop using your imagination to achieve your goals and fuel that passion. Don't let anyone talk you out of this dream or say it's impossible or that you can't make it as an actor. It is up to you to find the ways to ignite that passion and carry yourself forward. Many famous people have those stories about a parent, an Agent, a friend, a Producer, a Director, etc. who told them they would never make it in Hollywood. Did they listen to them? No!! They continued and fought through all the negatives and all the barriers that were thrown in their direction, came out the other side and ended up having very successful careers.

Life is up to you, go for it and never give up if it is your dream to be a successful actor or actress. PERSIST! PERSIST! PERSIST!

WORKSHEET:

GOALS:

These are just some examples - use your imagination and GO FOR IT!

In one month I will:

1. Do research for finding a community theater or acting class.

2. Start researching photographers in my area and talk to them about shooting my headshots.

3. Sit in on a couple of acting classes and find one you like and that you can afford.

In three months I will:

1. Be in a class

2. Audition for a play

3. Find two monologues and memorize them, etc.

4. Get my headshots done

In six months I will:

1. Get a part in a play

2. Make a list of local agents and managers who can come to see me

3. Put together a resume of performances I have done

4. Get appointments with agents and/or managers.

In one year I will:

1. Have been in at least one production

2. Have gotten an agent

3. Have gone on a professional interview

4. Have gotten a few callbacks

5. Have gone on-camera auditions

6. Have booked some professional jobs

In two years I will:

1. Be living in Los Angeles and going on auditions regularly.

2. Have gotten a job in a series as a regular or recurring.

3. Have done several good, independent movies.

After you've listed out the goals for yourself, examine each one and list out the actions it will take for you to achieve each one.

All of these activities could be accomplished well within a year or even less depending on how active and passionate you are on achieving your goals.

ABOUT THE AUTHOR

Lisa London is currently working as a Casting Director and principal of London/Stroud Casting.

Lisa has cast over fifty television shows, movies and pilots such as: *The Suite Life of Zack and Cody,* the pilot of *Hannah Montana, Mostly Ghostly, Roseanne, Ellen, Get A Life, Hit the Floor, Arli$$, Grandma's Boy, Stepfather,* and *House Bunny* to name a few.

Lisa has been a member of the CSA (Casting Society of America) for over twenty years.

You can view her credits at **imdb.com** or go to her website: **londonstroudcasting.com**

INDEX 1: LEGAL INFORMATION FOR MINORS

The following is information about requirements for anyone under the age of eighteen years old who wants to be in the Entertainment Industry.

Here is the info on how to get you started.

WORK PERMIT:

The first thing you are going to need is a Work Permit. This is a permit that anyone under the age of 18 must have to work in the Entertainment Industry unless you are "emancipated". Emancipation of a minor generally refers to the process of freeing a minor (person under age 18) from parental control. It means that the parent is no longer legally responsible for the acts of the child. It can allow the child to set up his/her own living arrangement. The term may also refer to freeing the earnings/income of a child from the control of a parent.

Procedure for obtaining a California Child Entertainment Work Permit

Application Form

An application form is included so you can see what it looks like. You can obtain an additional application form from any of the Division of Labor Standards Enforcement (DLSE) office or by visiting their website, **http://www.dir.ca.gov/dlse/.** If needed in a hurry, you can also go to their office in person. But go on the website first to see what you will need to bring with you in order to obtain the permit. There is also a Child Labor Law pamphlet that gives you all the information regarding how many hours your child can work, wages, permits and paperwork you will need, etc. Once obtained, the permit is good for six months of work and then must be renewed.

Parent or Guardian

Complete all requested information on the front of the application form, print, and sign your name where indicated.

School Record

This section must be completely filled out, signed, and stamped/sealed by an authorized school official (i.e. teacher, principal, guidance counselor, etc). If your school does not have an official "seal" or "stamp", please have them attach a letter, printed on official school letterhead stating that "your school does not have a seal or stamp, however this application form is still valid".

When school is IN SESSION, the application form must be completed and dated during the current school session by an authorized school official. The DLSE does not accept applications dated more than 30 days old.

When school is NOT IN SESSION, (i.e. spring break, vacation, holidays), either the minor's recent report card or letter from the school principal on school letterhead indicating that the minor is "satisfactory in all academic subjects, health and attendance" is required.

Home-schooled minors must show proof of enrollment in a home school program recognized by the minor's state of residence. Parents cannot simply sign their name as the child's home school teacher because additional information is required. If your state does not regulate home schooling, you must provide the DLSE with a copy of the laws governing home schooling in your state. Current employment law in California requires that you provide evidence that what you are doing is legal.

Non-School Age children are required to attach one of the following in lieu of completing the school record portion of the form:

a) Certified Birth Certificate

b) Baptismal Certificate

c) Official letter from hospital where born

d) Passport

Health Record

Infants under one month of age must have a licensed pediatric physician certify, "The infant is at least 15 days old, was carried to full term, and is physically able to endure the stresses of a film set."

Renewals:

To renew your permit, simply check the box on the application form marked renewal, attach a copy of your old permit and follow the instruction above.

Graduated Minor:

Minors who have graduated high school or have obtained a high school proficiency certificate do not need an entertainment work permit and should carry a copy of their diploma, GED or equivalence certificate with them in lieu of a work permit.

Sending Your Application

You have two options. Mail the application form to the DLSE or use a permit service.

DLSE PROCESSING—Free of Charge

You can send your permit directly to the DLSE office nearest you and your permit will be returned by mail free of charge. **You must include a preaddressed, stamped envelope with your application form**. Turnaround time is within three business days of receipt of your original application form by the DLSE. If your application form is incomplete it will be returned to you for corrections. The Labor Commission does not keep records of your Permit order. In the Los Angeles area, you can go to the Van Nuys office and there is a walk-in service that will process and renew permits. If you do not receive your permit within one month, you should call.

PERMIT SERVICE—Fee Applies

Children In Film is an independent service that can assist you in obtaining your permit for a fee. Call the Children In Film office toll free at 866/901–0082 for information and rates or visit their website **www.ChildrenInFilm.com**. Turnaround time to receive this permit may take 24 hours or more. Check with them if you are concerned about the wait.

Coogan Account Info:

In order for your child to work in show business in the state of California (and in some other states, too), you must have a special bank account set up for your child into which the money that he or she earns can be deposited.

Many years ago, there was a very successful child actor named **Jackie Coogan**. He first worked in vaudeville shows and in silent films, and then starred with **Charlie Chaplin** in the movie *The Kid* in 1921. Many other film roles for Jackie Coogan followed after that one, and he earned a substantial amount of money. Unfortunately, his mother and stepfather squandered nearly all the money he earned.

Jackie Coogan filed a lawsuit to get money back from them, but he only ended up getting a small portion of his actual earnings. It was this lawsuit that resulted in California legislation referred to as the *California Child Actor's Bill* (a.k.a. the Coogan Bill and the Coogan law). This law mandates that employers of a child actor or model deposit 15% of the money earned by that child into a special account called a **Coogan blocked trust account** (a.k.a. a Coogan trust fund, a Coogan trust account, or a Coogan account).

It is the responsibility of the parent or guardian of the child to set up this account for the child.

How do you set up a Coogan Trust Fund?

First, research financial institutions to find ones that have Coogan accounts. Find out how much the initial deposit has to be, and also be sure to check what the interest rate will be. In some banks, the account is a junior savings account that is blocked from withdrawals. This type of account typically has a very low interest rate. The SAG/AFTRA Credit Union often has the best rates and options for a Coogan account.

After choosing a financial institution, take your child's social security number and the money or a check for the initial deposit, and tell the bank to open a Coogan blocked trust account for your child with you as the trustee. It is a good idea to ask them exactly what documentation you need to open the account. Typically, they require a certified birth certificate for the child and proof of your identity (driver's license or passport). After opening the account, make sure to get a letter from the financial institution. This letter should have:

- the name, full street address, and phone number of the financial institution branch where the account was opened

- the date the account was opened

- the type of the account specified as a blocked trust account

- the routing number and account number

- the signature of the financial representative who set up the account

Immediately make several copies of this letter, filing the original at home and giving one to each of your child's talent representatives.

California law mandates that a work permit will be considered invalid if, within 10 days of issuance, a true and accurate copy of a Trustee Statement indicating the existence of a proper Coogan Blocked Trust Account is not attached. Enforcement of this continues to be hit and miss. However, the permits issued now have the following language printed ON them.

"Pursuant of California Labor Code Section 1308.9 (a). with respect to the employment of a minor under a contract described in Section 6750 of California Family Code, this permit shall be void after the expiration of 10 business days from the date hereof unless it is attached to a true and correct copy of the trustee's statement evidencing the establishment of a 'Coogan Trust Account' for the benefit of the minor named herein."

Parents will need to be prepared for what might potentially happen at the workplace, and be able to comply with this requirement.

When a child is employed in the entertainment industry, this information must be supplied to the employer so that the appropriate deposits can be made into the child's Coogan blocked trust account.

Since this account is a blocked trust, money can be deposited into the account, but no money can be withdrawn from this account by any person for any reason. Only the child can withdraw money from this account on or after his/her 18th birthday or when legally emancipated.

Emancipation:

Emancipated minors are those persons under 18 who possess a "Declaration of Emancipation" issued by the superior court. Minors declared emancipated by the court must be at least 14 years of age. Emancipated minors may apply for a Permit to Employ and Work without parental consent, but they are subject to all other child labor laws. They no longer have to have a teacher present on the set and are absolved from other parental guidelines while filming.

CHESPE Exam:

This is a California Proficiency Exam. If eligible to take the test, you can earn the legal equivalent of a high school diploma by passing the CHSPE. If you pass both sections of the CHSPE, the California State Board of Education will award you a Certificate of Proficiency, which by state law is equivalent to a high school diploma (although not equivalent to completing all coursework required for regular graduation from high school).

Requirements to take the exam:

He or she is at least 16 years old or he or she has been enrolled in the tenth grade for one academic year or longer.

If you pass this exam, you no longer need to have your parents or a guardian on the set with you and will no longer need a studio teacher to be provided for you. You will be allowed to work the same amount of hours as an adult actor.

IMPORTANT INFORMATION IF YOU ARE UNDER 18:

When you are under the age of 18 and still in school, there will be a teacher that is on the set. The teacher is responsible to make sure you stay up to date on your school work, so bring your school work with you to the set.

They are also there to insure the amount of time you are on camera does not exceed the state rules and that the production follows those rules. Of course, the younger you are, the less amount of time you get to be on camera. The following chart is for California production only. Please check in the state you will be shooting in for their requirements.

Hours of Work and Concurrent Requirements in California:

Age	Max Work Time	Education	Rest & Recreation	Meal Period	Total Time at Location
15 days to 5+ months	20 Min.	Maximum 100 ft. candle light, 30 sec exposure	N/A	N/A	2 hours
6 mo to 1+ years	2 hours	0	2 hours	.5 hour	4.5 Hours
2 years to 5+ years	3 hours	3 hours Education and R & R		.5 hour	6.5 hours
6 years to 8+ years	4 hours	3 hours	1 hour	.5 hour	8.5 hours
Non-school days	6 hours	0	1 hour	.5 hour	8.5 hours
9 years to 15+ years	5 hours	3 hours	1 hour	.5 hour	9.5 hours
Non-school days	7 hours	0	1 hour	.5 hour	9.5 hours
16 years to 17+ years	6 hours	3 hours	1 hour	.5 hour	10.5 hours
Non-school days	8 hours	0	1 hour	.5 hour	10.5 hours

Infants aged 15 days to 6 months may be at the place of employment for one period of two consecutive hours, which must occur between 9:30 a.m. and 11:30 a.m. or between 2:30 p.m. and 4:30 p.m. Actual work may not exceed 20 minutes under any circumstances.

Infants may not be exposed to light exceeding 100 foot-candles for more than 30 seconds at a time. A studio teacher and a nurse must be present for each three or fewer infants aged 15 days to 6 weeks. A studio teacher and a nurse must be present for each 10 or fewer infants aged 6 weeks to 6 months. A parent or guardian must always be present.

Minors aged 6 months to 2 years may be at the place of employment for up to four hours and may work up to two hours. The remaining time must be reserved for the minor's rest and recreation.

Minors aged 2 years to 6 years may be at the place of employment for up to six hours and may work up to three. The remaining time is reserved for the minor's rest and recreation.

Minors aged 6 years to 9 years when school is in session may be at the place of employment for up to eight hours, the sum of four hours work, three hours schooling and one hour of rest and recreation. When school is not in session, work time may be increased up to six hours, with one hour of rest and recreation.

Minors aged 9 years to 16 years when school is in session may be at the place of employment for up to nine hours, the sum of five hours work, three hours schooling and one hour of rest and recreation. When school is not in session, work time may be increased up to seven hours, with one hour of rest and recreation.

All minors aged 6 months to 16 years must be provided with one studio teacher for each group of ten or fewer minors when school is in session and for each group of twenty or fewer minors on Saturdays, Sundays, holidays or during school vacations. In addition to the studio teacher, a parent or guardian must always be present.

Exception: Minors under 16 do not require the presence of a studio teacher for up to one hour for wardrobe, make-up, hair-dressing, promotional publicity, personal appearances or audio recording if these activities are not on the set, if school is not in session *and* if the parent or guardian is present.

Minors aged 16 years to 18 years when school is in session may be at the place of employment for up to ten hours, the sum of six hours work, three hours schooling and one hour of rest and recreation. When school is not in session, work time may be increased up to eight hours, with one hour of rest and recreation. Studio teachers need only be present for the minors' schooling, if schooling is still required. A parent or guardian need not be present.

The time minors are permitted at the place of employment may be extended by no more than one-half hour for a meal period. All travel time between the studio and a location counts as work time. Up to forty-five minutes travel from on-location overnight lodging to a worksite is generally considered work time. Travel between school, home, and the studio is not work time.

You can download the current child labor laws in California from this website:

http://www.dir.ca.gov/DLSE/ChildLaborLawPamphlet.pdf

So you should have all the legal and administrative aspects handled now (contracts, Coogan Account, work permits, etc.) Now, it's on to the creative stuff!

Index 2: Additional Internet Resources

GENERAL INDUSTRY RESEARCH	
imdb.com	Internet movie database where you can look up professionals in the entertainment industry
imdbpro.com	Paid subscription version of the IMDB database provides more information and opportunity to promote yourself within the industry
ENTERTAINMENT NEWS	
backstage.com	Information on auditions, plus entertainment news, articles by successful actors and other industry professionals
deadline.com/hollywood	Entertainment industry news
Variety.com	Entertainment industry news
Hollywoodreporter.com	Entertainment industry news
Extratv.com	Celebrity news and gossip
accesshollywood.com	Celebrity news and gossip
eonline.com	Celebrity news and gossip
omg.yahoo.com/omg-insider	Celebrity news and gossip
FILM & TV PRODUCTION	
Mandy.com	Film and television production resources information, plus has casting notices
variety411.com	Production resources for LA & NY, plus has links for home rentals and leases
proactors.org	Lots of information on different acting resources includes links, acting school directories, photographers, etc.
YOUNG ACTORS RESOURCES	
bizparents.org	Provides education, and support to parents and children engaged in the entertainment industry
childreninfilm.com	Information on rules and regulations for kids and some casting notices
People.delphiforums.com/showtalk/	PARF is an information and discussion site for teens, young actors and parents of actors
THEATER INFORMATION	
playbill.com	Theater news and information
ibdb.com (internet broadway database)	Provides a comprehensive database of shows produced on Broadway
actorsequity.org	Actors & Stage Managers union also lists theatrical casting notices
NYCasting.com	Lists information regarding Agents, Managers, Casting Directors and audition notices in New York City

MISCELLANEOUS ORGANIZATIONS	
castingsociety.com	Casting Society of America - Research casting directors
emmys.com	Academy of Television Arts and Sciences
oscars.org	Academy of Motion Picture Arts and Sciences:
sagaftra.org	Screen Actors Guild website
SAGindie.com	Information on SAG independent movies and occasional casting notices
ONLINE AUDITION/SUBMISSION SITES	
Backstage.com	Lists of auditions and open casting calls in New York and LA
breakdownexpress.com	General information on breakdown services and Directories
actorsaccess.com	Subscribe to audition notices by region
castingnetworks.com	Subscribe to audition notices by region
thepeoplenetwork.com	Submission information for casting and agents
nowcasting.com	Submissions plus good info for actors
sfcasting.com	Submissions for projects casting in San Francisco area
castingfrontier.com	Submissions by region
cazt.com	Submission site for LA based actors
SIDES AND SCREENPLAYS	
showfax.com	Sides by major city or region
screenplayonline.com	Convenient screenplay access
simplyscripts.com	Links to hundreds of free, downloadable scripts
ACTOR & MANAGER INFO	
agentassociation.com	Association of Talent Agents: (list of talent agencies in Los Angeles and other cities)
talentmanagers.org	Talent Managers Association: (list of talent managers)
sagaftra.org/agency-relations/sag-franchised-agents	SAG/AFTRA Talent Agency's: (list of franchised & non-franchised agents)
GENERAL INFORMATION FOR ACTORS	
backstage.com/advice-for-actors/resources/los-angeles-acting-schools-and-coaches_6/	An excellent list of Los Angeles based acting schools and coaches

Index 3: NAVIGATING LOS ANGELES

Los Angeles is the 2nd most populated city in the United States. It extends over 40 miles from the desert to the ocean. It's huge and can seem impossible to find your way around. We'd like to help you with this. This chapter is by no means the end all for everything LA, but we will try to show you where much of the real action takes place.

We are not going to be telling you where all of the different casting offices are for a few different reasons. The main reason is that they change all the time. Many Casting Directors move their office locations with every new project they get. When we get a new show to cast, sometimes we are given space within the production offices and other times we are off site. Some Casting Directors do have more permanent offices and you would go see them at their office, no matter what show they are casting. But this is a constantly moving industry so it would be inaccurate to give any exact details about this. Definitely get a Casting Directory Guide which tells you where the Casting Directors are located, but make sure it is up to date. Before you go to a casting office, confirm their address so you make sure they haven't moved.

There are three major areas of Greater Los Angeles where a most of the studios and production facilities are located. The main ones are listed below:

HOLLYWOOD AREA	THE SAN FERNANDO VALLEY	CULVER CITY/CENTURY CITY/WEST LA
CBS Television City	ABC Family Channel	20th Century Fox
E! Entertainment TV	ABC Studios	BET Networks
Hollywood Center Studios	Cartoon Network	Comedy Central
Paramount Pictures	CBS Studio Center	Fox Broadcasting Company
Raleigh Studios	Disney Channel	HBO
Red Studios	Disney Studios	Lifetime TV
Sunset Gower Studios	Dreamworks	MGM
The Lot	NBC/Universal	MTV Networks
The Prospect Studios	Paramount Network TV	Showtime Networks
	The CW	Sony Pictures Entertainment
	Turner Broadcasting	Spike TV
	Universal Cable Productions	The Culver Studios
	Warner Brothers Studios	

Where you live is sometimes dependent on where you will be working consistently. But in terms of auditions, you could live anywhere. There are production offices, studios, Agents, Managers, and Casting Director's offices in many areas of Los Angeles. In terms of where to live, it is up to you to decide what works best for you and your family. For example, if you choose to be close to the Hollywood/Valley areas, there are a number of studios, and casting offices convenient to these locations. If your auditions happen to be in the Valley or Hollywood and you live on the west side—which includes the Culver City, Century City, Santa Monica and surrounding areas, it can be lots of additional driving and sitting on the famous Los Angeles freeways. If your auditions are on the West side and you live in those areas, then it will be less driving. The air is definitely cleaner near the beach and it's usually 10–20 degrees cooler. Definitely check out the different areas and decide what is the most convenient for your lifestyle.

We are listing a few places you can check out for living facilities when you come here. There are some that are completely furnished apartments with full kitchen facilities and then there are hotels like Extended Stay Los Angeles, depending on how long you are planning to be here. We are <u>not endorsing</u> any of the following places, we are just giving you some options to explore.

Living Facilities:

<u>The Oakwood Apartments</u>—**www.oakwood.com/tolucahills**

There is another Oakwood on the west side in Marina del Rey. These are very large facilities with hundreds of apartments; 1100 apartments in Toluca, 800 apartments in the Marina.

These are fully furnished studio, one and two bedroom apartments. They have a specialized program to assist child actors and their families who decide to come to Los Angeles to pursue their acting careers. Though we have never stayed there (because we live here), we have been told that staying at the Oakwood is very workable because it is convenient and they will rent by the week unless it is pilot season. But we have also been told by some moms, that it can become a bit of tough environment to handle, as everyone is watching what everyone else is doing and that it can get quite a bit competitive. Kids seem to like it though because they have a lot of pools and activities for them.

<u>1200 Riverside</u>—**www.liveat1200riverside.com**

Fully furnished studio and one bedroom residencies with kitchen facilities.

VRBO (Vacation Rentals by Owner)—**www.vrbo.com**

This is a website listing homes and apartments available for rent while the owners are away. It's usually in more of a suburban or urban neighborhood and gives you the feeling that you live there.

Home Away—**www.homeaway.com**

This is another online resource for finding a short term place to stay in Los Angeles that's not a hotel.

Actor's Sublet—**www.nycshortlease.com**

This is an online resource for actors going to New York.

Acting Teachers/Coaches:

There are a wide variety of acting schools and teachers in Los Angeles. It is best to get recommendations from Agents, Managers, friends, etc. If you don't have any resources to ask for this kind of assistance, then you will need to do your research online as best as you can. Call, ask your questions, see if you can possibly audit a class and keep searching till you find the best fit! I have included a link in the resource page that gives a big list of acting coaches and schools, but this isn't a complete list even though it is quite lengthy. Read the descriptions, get feedback and suggestions from people that you meet, make calls and check out a few that seem interesting to you.

Cars:

Either bring your own or if you are renting one, be sure it has GPS, or that you have a good maps app on your phone because you will need it. Los Angeles has many shortcuts and side streets that can get you to auditions besides the freeway. But this is a city of cars and traffic, so make sure you leave plenty of time to get to your audition. We do have a growing subway and above ground train system, but you would have to check out the times it runs and where it lets you off because it won't always be close to your auditions. It is definitely not as convenient as the New York subway system!

The following is a list of interesting places you could visit on your time off, or days free. Los Angeles is a beautiful city but it is so spread out it can seem intimidating to start off. Don't be afraid to get out and explore this city and the wonderful surrounding areas. We have everything from the arid dessert of Palm Springs to the beautiful beaches of Santa

Monica and Malibu, and more great beaches further north and south. Then there are the wonderful mountains just an hour and a half or more from downtown LA, including Lake Arrowhead and Big Bear. One of the most amazing parts of California is the coastline. With cities like, San Diego, San Clemente, San Capistrano, Huntington Beach, Newport Beach, Laguna Beach, and Dana Point, to name a few. Take a drive up or down the coast and enjoy the beautiful views. Of course, there are the tourist attractions that everyone has heard about including Disneyland, Knott's Berry Farm, Magic Mountain, Universal Studios, Grauman's Chinese Theater and Rodeo Drive. Take some day trips when you get a chance and enjoy your experience.

Places to Explore in Los Angeles:

Hikes:

- Fryman Canyon—good hiking
- Runyon Canyon—good hiking
- Lake Hollywood Reservoir Trail
- Griffith Park and Observatory—Light shows at the Planetarium
- Lake Shrine Temple—beautiful landmark with small lake and unbelievable landscaping

Shopping/Food:

- The Grove and the Farmer's Market—great for shopping, food and people watching
- The Americana in Glendale—also good for shopping and food
- 3rd Street Promenade in Santa Monica—great for an evening's stroll and people watching
- Venice Beach—on the weekends it's a real parade of unusual characters on foot and on roller skates.
- Main Street and Abbot Kinney—are great streets for unusual shops and great food.
- Montana Blvd—a cool street with high-end stores and food emporiums
- Old Town Pasadena—a great place for dinner on the weekends, as well as street musicians and good shopping
- Melrose Blvd—between Fairfax and Highland. More interesting neon signs in one place and good unique shops especially for those between the ages of twelve and twenty-five.
- The Fashion District and Santee Alley—great discount clothes with hawkers in front of every establishment.
- Larchmont—has fun restaurants and shops
- Toluca Lake—has good coffee shops, restaurants and some boutiques

- Los Feliz—fun village atmosphere with good coffee shops, restaurants and a few unique stores

Flea Markets:

- Rose Bowl Flea Market—takes place the 2nd Sunday of every month in Pasadena
- Fairfax Flea Market—every Sunday
- Farmer's markets—just check your internet for one near you. Fresh fruits, veggies and much more. These happen once a week in a number of different areas around the city.

Good Car Rides:

- Take Sunset Blvd all the way from downtown and stay on it all the way to the beach. You will see all of Los Angeles in its different manifestations.
- Mulholland Drive—famous from being in many movies and the views of the city and the Valley are spectacular.
- Bel-Air—access from Sunset Blvd and you can meander around and see estates that will blow your mind!
- Beverly Hills—driving up and down the streets is a great study in different kinds of architecture and landscaping that is great fun to see.
- Pacific Coast Highway (Highway 1) will take you to Santa Monica Beach and the Pier, Malibu Beach, Zuma Beach, and further south you'll find Manhattan Beach, Redondo Beach, Newport Beach, etc., all are worth exploring.

Downtown Los Angeles:

- Chinatown—fun to go downtown and have some Chinese food.
- Phillipe's—Home of the Original French Dip Sandwich
- The Last Bookstore—the largest independent bookstore in California that buys and sells used and new books and records. They also have musical and literary events.
- The downtown area is part of a huge resurgence of restaurants, galleries, bookstores, etc. You can find places that specialize in beer and sausage, and some of the newest cuisines ever, with prices that range from very expensive to very reasonable.

Hopefully, this gives you some information on Los Angeles and where to go to make the most of your experience while you are visiting or even if you decide to move here for a period of time. Once you get used to driving around LA, you will be a pro at getting where you need to go and knowing how much time it will take to get to auditions. Enjoy and take the time to explore and research this wonderful city!

CPSIA information can be obtained
at www.ICGtesting.com
Printed in the USA
LVOW04s1802090817
544393LV00007B/344/P